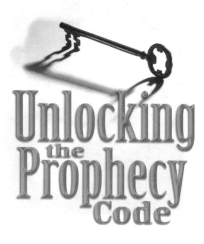

Unlocking
the
Prophecy
Code

BRYAN CUTSHALL

Foreword by Perry Stone

Unlocking
the
Prophecy
Code

Understanding Bible Mysteries in Types and Shadows

Book Editor: Wanda Griffith
Editorial Assistant: Tammy Hatfield
Copy Editors: Esther Metaxas
Julie E. McGuire

Library of Congress Catalog Card Number: 2005909652
ISBN: 1-59684-131-1
Copyright © 2005 by Pathway Press
Cleveland, Tennessee 37311
All Rights Reserved
Printed in the United States of America

DEDICATION

I dedicate each book I write to my wife,

Faith,

and our two daughters,

Brittany and
Lindsay.

They have been a part of every step of my journey. God has used them to teach me, encourage me and keep me on track. Their honesty, love, support and care are a constant strength to me. Their beauty alone is enough inspiration to wake up another day.

I also dedicate this book to a group of men who changed my life. Some years ago, a group of men in St. Louis asked me to mentor them. For several years, we met on the first Tuesday night of the month for discussion, growth, honesty and Bible study. During that time God taught me about the prophetic layers of Scripture. In my enthusiasm to share this new revelation, I began to teach these men what I knew. After a while, they were finding types and shadow codes before I was. We literally spent hours discussing the prophetic layer of Scripture. While I was a mentor to them, little did they know how much they became my teachers.

Our journey together eventually led us to a "rite of passage" trip in Honduras. There, we cut our way through the jungle and rode in dug-out canoes to reach the remote villages in the interior. For me, the greatest discovery of the trip was not the experience of the jungle, or even the rich memories of unity and friendship—it was that for hours every day we discussed the prophetic layer and unlocked rooms of treasure that were too rich for one person to hoard. These men went with me to the deep places where few dare to venture. I dedicate this book to our group of explorers who went on a spiritual safari to bring back an ancient prophetic treasure.

John Brandt

Kirk Jaudes

Don Moran

Al Piché

Larry Ridenour Jr.

Contents

Special Acknowledgments

Much of the credit for this project belongs to Andréa deCento, my administrative assistant and editor. She is an incredible wordsmith who has put a part of herself into editing each page. Her diligence, servitude and commitment to excellence have taken this book to a new caliber.

When I decided to write this book, we had to complete the manuscript in 28 days in order to meet our deadline. Andréa worked for hours editing each page until it sang. She is a gift to Faith and me, and as you read each page, you will see that she is also a gift to you.

Pastor Tony Landon agreed on short notice to write the discussion questions for each chapter. He is a brilliant scholar whom God has richly blessed with spiritual insight. For those who want to go deeper in the study, he has provided a thought-provoking journey for your delight and inspiration. As your group gathers to explore the chapters of *Unlocking the Prophecy Code*, you will be thankful that Pastor Landon took the time to help chart your course.

FOREWORD

It is a rare gift when the pastor of a large, growing, dynamic church has researched and discovered amazing prophetic insight, as has Bryan Cutshall. This is because most pastors must spend time dealing with everyday practical Christian living, and concentrate their efforts on keeping the flock in order. Dr. Cutshall, however, with his busy schedule, has taken precious time to tap into the unique insight by discovering key prophetic mysteries in the Bible by peeling away what he calls *prophetic layers*. By peeling away these layers, Dr. Cutshall unlocks numerous prophetic mysteries hidden within parables and stories of the Bible.

This method of research may be new to many in the Christian community, but it has been understood and practiced for centuries by Hebraic scholars and Jewish rabbis. Many rabbis teach that there are four levels of understanding the Scripture. The highest level is to unlock the mysteries hidden within the text.

This is the level you will discover when reading this new book. When reading *Unlocking the Prophetic Code*, I was reminded of Matthew 13:52: "Therefore every scribe which is instructed unto the kingdom of heaven is like unto a man that is an householder, which bringeth forth out of his treasure things new and old" (KJV).

It has been said that the Old Testament is the New Testament concealed, and the New Testament is the Old Testament revealed! Yet, within the inspired words of the Holy Bible are prophetic types, shadows, patterns and cycles. It is now time to understand and unlock the great prophetic mysteries for our generation, as spiritual knowledge is now being increased (Daniel 12:4). This book is part of a prophetic trail that leads to hidden treasure! "In whom are hidden all the treasures of wisdom and knowledge" (Colossians 2:3).

—Perry Stone
Founder of *Voice of Evangelism*
Host of *Manna-fest* Weekly Telecast

Introduction

I have been asked this question numerous times, "Why did God make the Bible difficult to understand?" Why didn't He just say it simply and remove the ambiguities? The answer lies in the following verses:

> He answered and said to them, "Because it has been given to you to know the mysteries of the kingdom of heaven, but to them it has not been given. For whoever has, to him more will be given, and he will have abundance; but whoever does not have, even what he has will be taken away from him. Therefore I speak to them in parables, because seeing they do not see, and hearing they do not hear, nor do they understand" (Matthew 13:11-13).

To him who has, more will be given and he will have abundance. This statement is not about materialism or money. It is about the knowledge of the Bible. This is a follow-up statement just after the parable of the sower was given—a parable about growing in the Word of God. The more of the Word we have inside of us, the more revelation we receive.

When a student of the Bible reads and rereads the Scriptures, it is as though imaginary lines begin to connect the passages to each other. All of a sudden, one passage will help you understand the one you just read. This process is the beginning of revelation. Connecting the passages is the key to understanding the matrix of the entire text. This divine book is truly interconnected. It is as if a spiritual ribbon is interwoven throughout the pages, allowing each passage to supernaturally connect to the next one.

Each time you uncover a mystery in Scripture, it makes you hungry for more. It can get as obsessive as craving your favorite food. Once revelation begins to flow, you can find yourself staying up for hours looking for more of the spiritual stepping-stones God laid out for you that lead to treasure houses of knowledge. My prayer is that *Unlocking the Prophecy Code* will whet your appetite for truth and leave you incomplete enough to want more.

Reading this book will be somewhat like going on a treasure hunt. The clues left for us by God will lead us on journeys that will fortify our beliefs, strengthen our faith and affirm our positions. Get ready to stretch, reach and grow as we learn how to understand mysteries and unlock the prophecy codes overlaid in types and shadows.

Now to Him who is able to establish you

according to my gospel

and the preaching of Jesus Christ,

according to the revelation of the mystery kept secret

since the world began but now made manifest,

and by the prophetic Scriptures made known to all nations,

according to the commandment of the everlasting God,

for obedience to the faith (Romans 16:25, 26).

1

UNLOCKING THE PROPHECY CODE

The closer we get to the return of Christ, the more we want to understand what His Word tells us regarding His return. I've heard many Christians say it's difficult to comprehend the prophetic layer of Scripture, and it *can* be. But picture this: Imagine a huge castle door that is locked. Strong men try to break it down using axes and picks; six or eight of them contrive to use a battering ram in an effort to breach its defense, to no avail. However, a child comes in carrying the key and is able to do what all those hulking men could not do—open the door.

The prophetic layer of Scripture can be difficult to comprehend, but we must realize that God *wants* us to understand it. That's why He gave us so many references within His Word. Jesus said He is the door. His Word provides the key.

Types and shadows are the unveiling of a mystery that has been imbedded in Scripture since the time of its inspiration.

Unlocking the Prophecy Code has to do with understanding how to recognize *types* and *shadows* in Scripture. However, it must be understood that this is not new revelation; types and shadows are the unveiling of a mystery that has been imbedded in Scripture since the time of its inspiration. Every book of the Bible is filled with them. I will explain types and shadows a little later in this chapter, but first there are several key scriptures that will help us understand their purpose.

> For we are members of His body, of His flesh and of His bones. "For this reason a man shall leave his father and mother and be joined to his wife, and the two shall become one flesh." This is a great mystery, but I speak concerning Christ and the church (Ephesians 5:30-32).
>
> . . . the mystery which has been hidden from ages and from generations, but now has been revealed to His saints. To them God willed to make known what are the riches of the glory of this mystery among the Gentiles: which is Christ in you, the hope of glory (Colossians 1:26, 27).
>
> And the disciples came and said to Him, "Why do You speak to them in parables?" He answered and said to them, "Because it has been given to you to know the mysteries of the kingdom of heaven, but to them it has not been given. For whoever has, to him more will be given, and he will have abundance; but whoever does not have, even what he has will be taken away from him" (Matthew 13:10-12).

These passages tell us that the Bible is filled with mysteries, but that we can understand them. According to Colossians 1:27, all of the mysteries are about one thing: Christ in you. Matthew 13:12 also gives us an important key to unlocking the mysteries. Unless you read the Bible regularly, you will never be able to understand these mysteries. When Matthew wrote, "For whoever has, to him more will be given, and he will have abundance; but whoever does not have, even what he has will be taken away from him," he was speaking about the Word of God.

If we have a basic foundation of Scripture, we will be able to understand other scriptures. If we do not, then what we do have, we will not remember. *It will be taken away* refers to the bird that comes and steals the seed from the field in the parable of the sower. The Bible tells us the birds are the wicked ones who will steal the Word from us, if we do not allow it to take root and grow. Romans 16:26 tells us that the mysteries of the Kingdom are revealed in the prophetic layer of the Scriptures. A fundamental knowledge of the Scriptures will assist you in understanding the prophetic layer. Later on, we will discuss the differences in the various layers of Scripture interpretation.

Two Key Words

There are two key words in understanding types and shadows—*concealed* and *revealed*. The mysteries have been *concealed* in the Scriptures, but *revealed* in the ministry and person of Jesus Christ. All types and

All types and shadows center around His life, His ministry, the salvation of mankind through Jesus as Messiah, the giving of the Holy Spirit to evangelize the world, and the return of Christ at the end of the age.

shadows center around His life, His ministry, the salvation of mankind through Jesus as Messiah, the giving of the Holy Spirit to evangelize the world, and the return of Christ at the end of the age.

What Is a Type?

Type is derived from the Greek term *tupos*, which occurs 16 times in the New Testament. It is translated various ways in the King James Version:

- ๐ Twice as *print* (John 20:25)
- ๐ Twice as *figure* (Acts 7:43; Romans 5:14)
- ๐ Twice as *pattern* (Titus 2:7; Hebrews 8:5)
- ๐ Once as *fashion* (Acts 7:44)
- ๐ Once as *manner* (Acts 23:25)
- ๐ Once as *form* (Romans 6:17)
- ๐ Seven times as *example* (1 Corinthians 10:6, 11; Philippians 3:17; 1 Thessalonians 1:7; 2 Thessalonians 3:9; 1 Timothy 4:12; 1 Peter 5:3).

Clearly these New Testament writers used the word *type* with some degree of latitude; yet one general idea is common to all: *likeness*—defined as "a person, event or thing fashioned to be a representation of something; an image."

A generation ago, a widespread interest in the study of types and shadows prevailed. Lately, the interest has subsided, primarily due to the extravagances of some writers who began to publish heresy. Because the subject was still under study, the average student was being confused. Doctrinal differences have always divided the body of Christ, and many modern-day writers used types to justify their doctrinal persuasion.

The Bible furnishes abundant evidence for the presence of types. A type is a comparison of two things—usually set up in a repeated Scriptural pattern. For instance, the story of Abraham taking Isaac to the mountain to be sacrificed is a type of Calvary. In both stories, there is the sacrificial son who bears the wood on his back up the hill. While it is not a replica of the story, nor does every fact line up, it bears the same pattern, and therefore leads us to a deeper understanding of the mysteries in Scripture. We will deal with this type later in the book. Other examples, like Abel as a type of Christ, or the rapture of Enoch as a type of the Rapture of the church, can help us to understand a Biblical pattern of events that highlight a main doctrinal event.

What Is a Shadow?

The word *shadow* is translated from the Greek word *skia*. In Hebrews 10:1, "For the law, having a shadow of the good things to come," it is as though the substance or reality that was still future cast its shadow backward into history. *Shadow* implies dimness and transitoriness, but it also implies a measure of resemblance between the one and the other.

While types generally refer to comparative patterns, shadows shed light on the future by connecting it to an event in the past.

While types generally refer to comparative patterns, shadows shed light on the future by connecting it to an event in the past. To understand this concept, let's compare it to our shadow when standing in sunlight. Our shadow is always attached to us, starting at our feet. Depending upon the position of the sun, it can be seen in front of us, at our side, or behind us. Biblical shadows are the same. The person in the Biblical shadow is Christ. The shadows may be found behind Him (reflecting a time in history) or in front of Him (reflecting the future), but they are always attached to His feet.

OTHER WORDS THAT SHARE THE GENERAL IDEA

The Definition of Parable

Matthew 13:34 says, "All these things Jesus spoke to the multitude in parables; and without a parable He did not speak to them." A parable is a short, simple story designed to communicate a spiritual truth, religious principle, or moral lesson. It has also been defined as a figure of speech in which truth is illustrated by a comparison or example drawn from everyday experiences. It is often no more than an extended metaphor or simile, using figurative language in the form of a story to illustrate a particular truth. The word *parable,* translated from the Greek word *parabole,* literally means "a laying by the side of, or a casting alongside," thus *a comparison or likeness.* According to *Nelson's Illustrated Bible Dictionary,* in a parable, something is placed alongside something else in order that one may throw light on the other.

The Definition of Copy

The word *copy* or *pattern,* from the Greek word *hupodeigma,* denotes a sketch or draft of something future or invisible, as in Hebrews 9:23. The Tabernacle and its furniture and services were copies, outlines of heavenly things.

Unlocking the Code

A better understanding of types and shadows gives us the key to unlocking the prophecy code. Eschatology is one of the most controversial subjects in Christendom. However, a better understanding of the repeated Biblical patterns sheds a whole new light on the subject. One of the reasons for the confusion is that so many people have created a major doctrine from their own understanding of a few scriptures. While some of those scriptures do provide a window to look into the past, present and

Types and shadows offer a repeating Biblical pattern that is like following a trail of bread crumbs to a major event.

future, many of those windows only give perspective from one angle.

The key to understanding is viewing a particular scripture from as many angles as possible. Each time the pattern is repeated, you gain new insight about the event. Types and shadows offer a repeating Biblical pattern that is like following a trail of bread crumbs to a major event. The key to translating the meaning of parables and mysteries in Scripture comes from a broader understanding of types and shadows.

Questions for Discussion

1. What are the two key words for unlocking the prophecy code?

2. How many books in the Bible contain types and shadows?

3. Are *types* and *shadows* a source of new revelation?

4. What are some scriptures that help to develop an understanding of types and shadows?

5. What is the central theme of each of the Bible mysteries?

6. Define and explain *type.*

7. Define and explain *shadow.*

8. Discuss the Biblical use of parables.

9. How are parables, types, shadows and copies useful in unmasking hidden truth?

10. Why is the discovery of Biblical patterns so vital?

Then He spoke many things to them in parables, saying:

"Behold, a sower went out to sow. And as he sowed,

some seed fell by the wayside;

and the birds came and devoured them.

Some fell on stony places,

where they did not have much earth;

and they immediately sprang up

because they had no depth of earth.

But when the sun was up they were scorched,

and because they had no root they withered away.

And some fell among thorns,

and the thorns sprang up and choked them.

But others fell on good ground and yielded a crop:

some a hundredfold, some sixty, some thirty.

He who has ears to hear, let him hear!"

(Matthew 13:3-9).

2

THE DECODER KEYS

God is a God of precision. He is not simply giving us illustration in principle, but rather, illustration in detail. Since we know that every parable contains a mystery that needs to be unlocked, we must ask if there are any clues in the Scripture that will help us unlock them correctly. When we unlock one mystery, the symbols unveiled will serve as decoders for the other parables.

First Things First

Jesus interpreted two of His parables—the Parable of the Sower and the Parable of the Wheat and the Tares—to help His disciples comprehend the parabolic teachings. The types and shadows Jesus revealed in these two parables remain consistent. To understand the other parables, it is important to take the symbols He revealed and utilize them as the decoder keys. Let's start our journey.

THE PARABLE OF THE SOWER

Then He spoke many things to them in parables, saying: "Behold, *a sower* went out to sow. And as he sowed, some *seed* fell by the *wayside*; and the *birds* came and devoured them. Some fell on *stony places*, where they did not have much earth; and they immediately sprang up because they had *no depth of earth*. But when the sun was up they were scorched, and because they had no root they withered away. And some fell among *thorns*, and the thorns sprang up and choked them. But others fell on *good ground* and yielded a *crop*: some a hundredfold, some sixty, some thirty. He who has ears to hear, let him hear!" (Matthew 13:3-9, emphasis added).

The Interpretation

"Therefore hear the parable of the sower: When anyone *hears the word of the kingdom*, and does not understand it, then *the wicked one* comes and snatches away what was sown in his heart. *This is he who received seed by the wayside.* But he who received the seed on stony places, this is he who *hears the word and immediately receives it with joy; yet he has no root in himself, but endures only for a while.* For when tribulation or persecution arises because of the word, immediately he stumbles. Now he who received seed among *the thorns is he who hears the word, and the cares of this world and the deceitfulness of riches choke the word, and he becomes unfruitful.* But he who received seed on the *good ground is he who hears the word and understands it, who indeed bears fruit* and produces:

some a hundredfold, some sixty, some thirty"
(Matthew 13:18-23, emphasis added).

The Decoder Keys

O *Sower*—a minister who gives the Word of
   the Kingdom

O *Ground*—the human race

O *Wayside*—people who hear the Word but do
   not understand it, because they have no
   Word in them

O *Birds*—Satan and wicked people

O *Stony places*—people who receive the Word
   with joy, but *have no root* in themselves

O *Thorns*—people who hear the Word, but are
   entangled in the cares of life and the quest
   to make money

O *Good ground*—he who hears the Word and
   understands it because he has the Word
   in him

O *Crops*—fruit in the life of a Christian

THE PARABLE OF THE
WHEAT AND THE TARES

Another parable He put forth to them, saying:
"The kingdom of heaven is like *a man* who *sowed
good seed* in his *field*; but while men slept, his
enemy came and sowed *tares* among the *wheat*
and went his way. But when the grain had

sprouted and produced *a crop*, then the tares also appeared. So the *servants of the owner* came and said to him, 'Sir, did you not sow good seed in your field? How then does it have tares?' He said to them, 'An enemy has done this.' The servants said to him, 'Do you want us then to go and gather them up?' But he said, 'No, lest while you gather up the tares you also uproot the wheat with them. Let both grow together until *the harvest*, and at the time of harvest I will say to the reapers, "First gather together the tares and bind them in bundles to burn them, but gather the wheat into my *barn*"'" (Matthew 13:24-30, emphasis added).

The Interpretation

Then Jesus sent the multitude away and went into the house. And His disciples came to Him, saying, "Explain to us the parable of the tares of the field." He answered and said to them: "*He who sows the good seed is the Son of Man. The field is the world,* the *good seeds are the sons of the kingdom,* but the *tares are the sons of the wicked one. The enemy who sowed them is the devil,* the *harvest is the end of the age,* and the *reapers are the angels.* Therefore as the tares are gathered and burned in the *fire,* so it will be at the end of this age. The Son of Man will send out His angels, and *they will gather out of His kingdom all things that offend, and those who practice lawlessness,* and will cast them into the furnace of fire. There will be wailing and gnashing of teeth.

As the tares are gathered and burned in the fire, so it will be at the end of this age.

Then the righteous will shine forth as the sun in the kingdom of their Father. He who has ears to hear, let him hear!" (vv. 36-43, emphasis added).

The Decoder Keys

- ❶ *A man*—the Son of Man (Jesus)

- ❶ *Field*—the world

- ❶ *Wheat seeds*—sons of the Kingdom

- ❶ *Tares*—sons of the Wicked One

- ❶ *Enemy*—the devil

- ❶ *Harvest*—end of the age

- ❶ *Reapers*—angels

- ❶ *Gathering of the tares*—evil people will be taken out of the world at the second coming of Christ

- ❶ *Fire*—hell

- ❶ *Barn*—millennial kingdom

USING THE DECODER KEYS

Now that we have a few keys, we can use them to find new keys and start unlocking the mysteries of other parables. To gain the broadest and most complete understanding of Scripture, it is important to look at it through a telescope instead of a microscope.

To gain the broadest and most complete understanding of Scripture, it is important to look at it through a telescope instead of a microscope.

Using a microscope to interpret the mysteries of Scripture will lead to heresy. We must not take one decoder key and use it to misinterpret scriptures when the rest of the passage does not line up with other doctrinal truths. Even if you think you are on to something, do not believe it or teach it unless you can find the pattern in other passages to support your theory. Throughout history, entire denominations have been formed on heresy. It is possible to get thousands of people to believe a lie if they do not have a good foundation in Scripture and theology.

With a microscope, you focus on a tiny component of the whole, whereas with a telescope, you stand far away and look at it from a broader, more complete vantage point. The key to knowing you have correctly interpreted the mystery is that it will be found in other patterns and, most of the time, will be repeated over and over.

We will use the decoder keys to bring new light on a tiny parable that is often misinterpreted.

The Parable of the Mustard Seed

Another parable He put forth to them, saying: "The kingdom of heaven is like a *mustard seed*, which *a man* took and sowed in *his field*, which indeed is the least of all the *seeds*; but when it is grown it is greater than the herbs and becomes a tree, so that the *birds* of the air come and nest in its branches" (Matthew 13:31, 32, emphasis added).

The Mustard Seed

To interpret this parable correctly, we have to realize that the illustrations Christ used were both common and practical. Even though the Jewish listeners did not understand the Kingdom analogy, they certainly understood the content of the story. Therefore, we must first draw attention to the *grain of mustard seed*.

Verse 32 of our text calls it "the least of all the seeds." The sower in this parable is simply called *a man*. However, it does call the field "his field." In the Parable of the Sower, we have already identified the owner of the field as Christ. According to the progression of the story, this is not the same seed sown earlier. The verbiage of this text says that the man *took* the seed and *sowed* it. We know then that it was added to the wheat field. Consequently, we must ask the question, "What is the purpose of sowing an additional type of seed in the field?" The wheat, as we know, is the Word of God. Why does the field need more than the Word?

At first glance, it appears as though the owner is adding mustard to the wheat field. If this is true, we could possibly conclude that adding the mustard to the wheat field is adding faith to the Word, which we know is necessary. Jesus uses the mustard seed as an illustration to teach about faith. While the Word of God can stand alone by its own authority and merit, we do need faith to accept and believe the Word.

The Tree

The next part of the passage captures my attention the most. Mustard is an herb, which grows into a shrub very slowly. The seed in this parable produces a tree, not a small plant that grows rapidly. There are two types of mustard plants. One grows to be about 18 inches in height, while the other one can reach up to 6 feet tall, looking very much like a tree.

When faith has been added to the Word, it accelerates our growth. However, the next part of this parable gives a warning to those who walk by faith and not by sight. "Word-carrying believers" stand on the promises in God's Word. Because they walk by faith and not by sight, they have to keep their eyes on the promises and not on the cares of life surrounding them. It is the Word and the faith that carries them through the battle.

The Birds

In the Parable of the Sower, the birds of the air are interpreted as Satan coming to steal the Word that falls upon a stony heart. In the parable of the mustard seed, verse 32 says the birds actually live in the tree or lodge in its branches. Those who operate in word and faith need to understand that the birds are always waiting to steal the seed from their mouths. We sow our words of faith in what we say. We either speak life or death.

Ephesians 2:2 says, "You once walked according to the course of this world, according to the prince of the power of the air, the spirit who now works in the sons of disobedience."

If you look up the words *of the air* in a Bible concordance, every reference but this one will read, "the birds of the air." The Greek word for *air* used in the passage is also translated as "breath." If Satan is the prince and power of the air, then he has to wait for us to speak, in order to have ammunition. If the only ammunition he has is what we say, how much more important it is for us to walk by faith and not by sight. We must learn to *talk* by faith and say what God says. Flippant conversations that seem innocent can be turned into verbal whirlwinds when Satan and wicked people twist the words to try to discount the speaker and the Word of God.

Flippant conversations that seem innocent can be turned into verbal whirlwinds when Satan and wicked people twist the words to try to discount the speaker and the Word of God.

David prayed a prayer that we too need to pray. It is found in Psalm 141:3, 4:

> Set a guard, O Lord, over my mouth; keep watch over the door of my lips. Do not incline my heart to any evil thing, to practice wicked works with men who work iniquity; and do not let me eat of their delicacies.

We must not forget that the kingdom of God on this earth is well-documented in the seven letters to the seven churches, given by John in the Revelation. Even as it tells of a glorious, overcoming body, each letter also warns of pitfalls. While the kingdom of God on this earth is filled with victory, triumphant battles, and incredible stories of deliverance and faith, we are also forewarned of those who will try to attack the Kingdom and use the Word of God in their attack. There is already a great attack against the authenticity and validity of the Word. Those of us who believe it should know how to defend it and not allow our words to be used to discount our beliefs.

The Word of God is essential to spiritual maturity and growth. It must not be compromised in any way, especially in the name of crowds or monetary gain. In a day when people do not want to hear sound doctrine, it is more important than ever to stand for the true Word of the Lord.

Questions for Discussion

1. What two parables did Jesus interpret for His disciples?

2. How can we benefit from studying the Parable of the Sower and the Parable of the Wheat and the Tares?

3. List and explain the decoder keys in the Parable of the Sower.

4. List the decoder keys in the Parable of the Wheat and the Tares. Discuss the revealed message.

5. What type of examination is necessary for a more complete understanding of Scripture, *microscopic* or *telescopic*? Explain.

6. Why is it imperative to discover Biblical patterns in the study of the Word as it relates to decoder keys?

7. Whom does the man represent in the Parable of the Mustard Seed?

8. In this parable, who owns the field?

9. What does the wheat represent?

10. What is the purpose of the addition of the mustard seed to the wheat field?

*And behold, a certain lawyer stood up and tested Him, saying,
"Teacher, what shall I do to inherit eternal life?" He said to him,
"What is written in the law? What is your reading of it?"
So he answered and said, "'You shall love the Lord your God
with all your heart, with all your soul, with all your strength,
and with all your mind,' and 'your neighbor as yourself.'" And
He said to him, "You have answered rightly; do this and you will
live." But he, wanting to justify himself, said to Jesus,
"And who is my neighbor?" Then Jesus answered and said:
"A certain man went down from Jerusalem to Jericho,
and fell among thieves, who stripped him of his clothing,
wounded him, and departed, leaving him half dead.
Now by chance a certain priest came down that road.
And when he saw him, he passed by on the other side.
Likewise a Levite, when he arrived at the place,
came and looked, and passed by on the other side.
But a certain Samaritan, as he journeyed, came where he was.
And when he saw him, he had compassion.
So he went to him and bandaged his wounds, pouring on oil and
wine; and he set him on his own animal, brought him to an inn,
and took care of him. On the next day, when he departed,
he took out two denarii, gave them to the innkeeper,
and said to him, 'Take care of him; and whatever more you spend,
when I come again, I will repay you.' So which of these three
do you think was neighbor to him who fell among the thieves?"
And he said, "He who showed mercy on him." Then Jesus said
to him, "Go and do likewise"*
(Luke 10:25-37).

3

THE GOOD SAMARITAN
OR THE RETURNING MESSIAH?

In Luke 10, a strange mixture appears in Scripture for the first time: oil and wine. We have seen them used many times, but never together. What is the purpose of this medicinal mixture that was poured into the wounds of a dying man? Is it an ancient apothecary practice, or does it have a deeper spiritual meaning? To understand this mystery, we must unlock the code on the prophetic layer of Scripture by finding the clues.

The setting of this oil-and-wine mixture is found in the Parable of the Good Samaritan. Before we get into the text, let's review the setting. What prompts the parable is a question posed by a Jewish lawyer. It is important to understand that this was not the same kind of lawyer we have in our modern culture. Rather, this was an expert in the religious customs; one who debated the Mosaic Law. The law in question here is not a civil code, but rather the Law of the Torah. The question asked was, "What must I do to inherit eternal life?" Jesus simply replied, "What is written in the Law, and how do you understand it?" The debater summed up the Law correctly by stating the Great Commandment as his answer. However, he pressed in to test the Lord by asking, "Who is my neighbor?"

Typically in our world, a neighbor is one who lives in our community. But Jesus and the man asking the question knew that just doing good in the community would not guarantee eternal life. Jesus gave him a much deeper answer than he could comprehend, and by doing so, He left a mystery to be unfolded later when revelation knowledge would be poured out in the body of Christ.

THE PARABLE OF THE GOOD SAMARITAN

And behold, a certain lawyer stood up and tested Him, saying, "Teacher, what shall I do to inherit eternal life?" He said to him, "What is written in the law? What is your reading of it?" So he answered and said, " 'You shall love the Lord your God with all your heart, with all your soul, with all your strength, and with all your mind,' and 'your neighbor as yourself.' "

And He said to him, "You have answered rightly; do this and you will live." But he, wanting to justify himself, said to Jesus, "And who is my neighbor?" Then Jesus answered and said: "A certain man went down from Jerusalem to Jericho, and fell among thieves, who stripped him of his clothing, wounded him, and departed, leaving him half dead. Now by chance a certain priest came down that road. And when he saw him, he passed by on the other side. Likewise a Levite, when he arrived at the place, came and looked, and passed by on the other side. But a certain Samaritan, as he journeyed, came where he was. And when he saw him, he had compassion. So he went to him and bandaged his wounds, pouring on oil and wine; and he set him on his own animal, brought him to an inn, and took care of him. On the next day, when he departed, he took out two denarii, gave them to the innkeeper, and said to him, 'Take care of him; and whatever more you spend, when I come again, I will repay you.' So which of these three do you think was neighbor to him who fell among the thieves?" And he said, "He who showed mercy on him." Then Jesus said to him, "Go and do likewise" (Luke 10:25-37).

This powerful parable not only answers the question about eternal life, but it gives the salvation story from beginning to end—starting with Adam and ending with the second coming of Christ, when He sets up His millennial kingdom on this earth.

The first clue given is the continual use of one word—*certain*. He is revealing that if we can identify the characters in the story, we can understand the meaning of the parable. He uses the phrase three times:

- ○ "A certain man went down from Jerusalem to Jericho."

- ○ "A certain priest came down that road."

- ○ "A certain Samaritan . . . came where he was."

A Certain Man

The key to unlocking this code is identifying the individuals named here. Since we are speaking in spiritual analogies, we must first identify the one who left Jerusalem and went down to Jericho. Jerusalem is always identified in Scripture as the place where God dwells. It is first identified in Scripture as the city of Salem, under the rulership of King Melchizedek (Genesis 14). *Salem* means "City of Peace." It was cap-

tured by the Jebusites and became *Jebus-Salem*, which was later shortened to one word—*Jerusalem*. The New Jerusalem will be the city of our God. Therefore, we are looking for a place where God dwells.

Jerusalem is always identified in Scripture as the place where God dwells.

Next, we must identify why Jericho, the city where the walls fell, was used in the story. Jericho was the first city in the Canaan land, which at the time was the land of their enemy that had to be conquered and possessed. Later, in the time of Jesus, Jericho was known as the wicked city.

The mountain overlooking Jericho is where Satan came to Jesus and tempted Him. Satan pointed out his domain in Jericho and offered it to Christ if He would bow down and worship him. Consequently, Jericho is easily identified as the place of this world under Satan's domain. Now it is easy to see why the story says this man went *down* to Jericho.

In order to identify the *certain* man, we must look for a man who was in the dwelling place of God but went down to the world's system into the domain of Satan. If we are looking for a man, it seems logical to start with the first man to find out who fits the description. We begin and end our search with Adam, for it is easy to see that he was the first man who lived in the dwelling place of God—a place known as *Eden*, which literally means "pleasure." It was he who left the Paradise which God had created for him and went down into Satan's domain. Adam's sin was disobedience. God told him that he could eat from every fruit tree in the Garden except one. That one tree was God's, constituting the tithe of the Garden, or that part that belonged to God. Adam did not physically die when he ate the forbidden fruit, but he did die spiritually. Adam is now half-dead, just as the parable states.

He is physically alive, yet spiritually dead. The thief who robbed him is Satan. Not only is the man spiritually dead, or half-dead, he is also stripped. The first thing Adam realized after he sinned was that he was naked. Adam had been clothed each day in innocence and did not need clothing. But now that he is living in sin, he sees his own nakedness and is ashamed. Sin will not only separate you from God, but it will also make you see yourself differently.

Before we go on, let's review what we have already learned about this parable:

Sin will not only separate you from God, but it will also make you see yourself differently.

Then Jesus answered and said: "A *certain man* [Adam] went down from *Jerusalem* [Garden of Eden] to *Jericho* [the world and the sinful life] and fell *among thieves* [Satan and his demons], who *stripped him of his clothing* [Adam knew he was naked when he sinned], wounded him, and departed, leaving him *half dead* [physically alive but spiritually dead]" (Luke 10:30).

A Certain Priest

All we know about the priest is that he came down that road. We can assume it is either a man who walked the Jericho road between Jerusalem and Jericho or a man who walked the spiritual road of being robbed and left half-dead. It seems that the best place to start is the beginning of the priesthood. The word *priest* literally means "one who officiates in religious services."

The first mention of a priest was Melchizedek. Yet Melchizedek has no beginning or end, and therefore does not fit our description. There are other priests mentioned for other religions, but the next priest of God mentioned is Moses. Moses was chosen by God to establish the Levitical priesthood through his older brother, Aaron, and Aaron's four sons. Even though Aaron is mentioned as the first high priest of the Levitical order, it was Moses who performed all of the religious mediation for the people. It was Moses who brought the Law of God from the mountain to the people. It was Moses who led them out of slavery, took them through the wilderness, brought miracles, and set up the civil code of order. Not only was Moses the first priest, he appeared with the great prophet Elijah on the Mount of Transfiguration. These two represent the offices of priest and prophet. There is no doubt that Moses fits the description of the priest for which we are searching.

In order to identify Moses more clearly as the priest, we must see if he lived out the story given to us in this parable. First of all, he had to come down that road. Even though Moses was born into a slave family, he grew up in the palace because of the favor of God. While other children were being slaughtered, God provided a way for him to be spared. Yet, even though he was a prince, he fled the land of his birth and hid away in the desert for 40 years as a fugitive. Moses was *stripped* of his royal garments and left

Egypt half-dead. He was alive, but he could not return home. It was not until the burning-bush experience, when Moses was 80 years old, that he began to talk to God again. He was alive, but spiritually, he was a dead man.

If Moses is the priest we're looking for, why does he pass by on the other side? Adam's wound was a spiritual wound. Sin had separated mankind from God by leaving them spiritually dead. The only cure was to revive them spiritually. Moses was given the Law of God to identify sin, but he was not given a cure for removing sin. Therefore, as the priest approached the sinful man lying on the road, he could not help him. He had to walk around him, because he had no means of restoring him spiritually.

Moses was given the Law of God to identify sin, but he was not given a cure for removing sin.

The Levite

Aaron became the first high priest given to restore man back to God by substitutionary sacrifices. Animals were killed and sacrificed to cover their sins. God accepted the blood and death of the animals as a substitute for the wages of sin. An animal was killed to cover the bodies of Adam and Eve. While it covered their bodies, it did not remove their sin. The Levites could only remove the sins of the people one at a time, but they could do nothing about their inherent sinful nature. Once sin was identified, it created a cycle of guilt because man could not keep himself from sinning.

So even though the Levite could assist man in his struggle with sin, he had no way of restoring sinful man back to God. Only the high priest could approach God, and then only on the Day of Atonement after a rigorous ritual of washing, fasting, cleansing and personal rededication. Even though he approached God on behalf of the people, the people themselves were left outside, separated from God by a veil, living in the fear of dying in their sins. Therefore, the Levite looked at the plight of man. Because he could do nothing to cure his sinful state, he had to walk on around him.

> Now by chance a *certain priest* came down *that road* [Moses, the first of the priests]. And when he saw him, *he passed by on the other side* [the Law could not remove sin]. Likewise a *Levite* [the ordinance of the sacrifices through the Levitical priests], when he arrived *at the place* [the sacrifices could not permanently remove sin], *came and looked*, and passed by on the other side [tried to remove sin, but could not] (vv. 31, 32).

A Certain Samaritan

In order to identify the Samaritan in the parable, we must first understand what constitutes a Samaritan citizen. When the kingdoms of Israel and Judah were divided during the times of the kings, Jerusalem remained the capital of Judah and Samaria became the capital of Israel. Samaria was made up of Hebrew people from 10 of the tribes of Israel. Later, when the 12 tribes were reunited by the Lord, they were instructed to put away their strange wives and stop mixed breeding. God wanted them to remain a pure race of people in order to preserve their religion, language, land and heritage. The Samaritans refused to do so; thus they became known as half-breeds and outcasts to the rest of the Jewish people. Therefore, a Samaritan is a person who has one Jewish parent and one parent of a different bloodline.

While it would be impossible to survey all the Samaritans in history, we must remember that this story is a spiritual analogy and must not be read in a literal sense, or the mystery can never be revealed. We are searching for a person who has one Jewish parent and one parent of another bloodline, in a spiritual sense.

Since we are searching for a spiritual man, the only person in history who would fit this description is Jesus. Jesus was the son of two parents. His Father was the Holy Spirit and His mother was a Jewish virgin named Mary. He was half Jewish and yet He possessed the one thing Adam and all who followed needed the most—a spirit that was alive. Jesus was the only One who could restore fallen and sinful man back to God.

The Samaritan came to where the wounded man was, just as Jesus came from heaven to earth for the sole purpose of redeeming mankind back to God. As we see the Samaritan approaching the half-dead man on the side of the road, we will see God's plan unfold for man's salvation and restoration. The first thing the Samaritan does is pour in oil and wine. Never before in Scripture has this mixture existed. This chapter opens up questions regarding this strange apothecary combination. Certainly, no one would think of pouring such a mixture into an open wound. Why does the parable use this strange concoction?

The Oil

Oil has long been celebrated as a symbol of the Holy Spirit in the following ways:

- Poured on the heads to anoint priests
- Poured on stones to anoint and sanctify rooms
- Poured on dirt to sanctify the ground
- Used to identify the presence of God

God chose oil as a tangible illustration to exemplify the power and working of the Holy Spirit. Oil causes a lamp to burn and give light, just as the Holy Spirit causes a person to burn with passion and give light. Oil causes one to glow and give off the aroma of anointing. In the same way, the Holy Spirit causes our lives to be changed and offers the aroma of our worship as a continual burning incense to God. Oil, as a lubricant, gives easy movement and flow in the same

The Holy Spirit causes our lives to be changed and offers the aroma of our worship as a continual burning incense to God.

manner that the anointing of the Holy Spirit causes things to flow.

The Wine

Wine was considered nothing more than a drink until Christ identified His blood with it in the Jewish Seder celebration during the Feast of Passover. This meal, often referred to as the *Holy Supper* or *Last Supper*, gives us an illustration never used before. As the disciples took the cup of wine from our Lord, He said, "This cup is the new covenant in My blood. This do, as often as you drink it, in remembrance of Me" (1 Corinthians 11:25). The wine is now identified as the blood of Jesus.

When you combine this mixture, you see that the Samaritan was pouring in the Holy Spirit and the blood of the sacrificial Lamb of God. This alone could restore mankind to God. The outpouring of the Holy Spirit would revive his spirit, and the blood of Jesus would remove all of his sins—including past sins he could not confess or even remember.

The Animal

The Samaritan picked up the wounded man and placed him on his own animal. There is no record of the type of animal mentioned here. That is insignificant, because in the spiritual analogy, the animal was not an animal at all. Instead it is a type of every animal that had been sacrificed for centuries, foreshadowing the day the Lamb of God would be sacrificed on a cross. Millions of animals had died for the sins of man.

The vicarious death gave man hope, but every drop of animal blood that had ever been shed since the first animal was killed in the Garden could not do for man what the first drop of blood did on Calvary's hill. Never before had a sinless spiritual man been offered as a sacrifice to pay for mankind's sin. Because Jesus was sinless, His royal blood cleansed mankind of all sin, so much so that the veil in the Temple that separated God from man was rent in two. Mankind has been restored to God through the shedding of the blood of Jesus and the giving of the Holy Spirit.

Because Jesus was sinless, His royal blood cleansed mankind of all sin, so much so that the veil in the Temple that separated God from man was rent in two.

The Inn and the Innkeeper

It is now easy to see how Jesus answered the question, "What must I do to inherit eternal life?" But He didn't stop with the removal of man's sins and the reviving of his spiritual state. Jesus provides the completion of man's total restoration.

Next, He tells us that the man is taken to an inn so that he can completely heal from his near-death experience. The Samaritan takes him there and leaves him with the innkeeper. This isn't the first time we hear a story of Jesus being associated with an inn, but it's the *only* other time besides the time of His birth. At no other time in Jesus' ministry is there mention of Him visiting an inn. The only thing said of the inn at the time of His birth is that there was no room for Him.

Later on, when John gives the seven letters to the seven churches of Asia Minor, we hear of another place that had no room for Christ. That place is the church. To the Laodicean church He says, "Behold, I stand at the door and knock. If anyone hears My voice and opens the door. . ." (Revelation 3:20). It's no coincidence that this takes place in the last church age preceding His return.

The inn in this parable characterizes the church, and the innkeeper represents the ministers of the church. Jesus takes the plight of sinful man and places it in the hands of His church. He commissions the church to reach sinful man in the same way He did. He wants the church to reach out to a spiritually dead mankind and pour in the oil and wine. Jesus is identifying the neighbor as anyone who is in need of salvation. He is instructing us to go find the lost and proclaim the salvation story; and when the Holy Spirit, the agent of salvation, indwells them, they will be alive for the first time.

"When I Come Again"

The Samaritan took the wounded man to the inn and paid the innkeeper two denarii. At first glance, this seems insignificant, but according to Matthew 20, in the parable of the workers in the vineyard, a denarii is one day's wage. It seems as though the innkeeper was paid to take care of the wounded man for two days. For the spiritual analogy, we go to an emphatic statement to the church in 2 Peter 3:8: "Beloved, do not forget this one thing, that with the Lord one day is as a thousand years, and a thousand years as one day." He said this in the middle of a lesson he was teaching on the coming of the Lord. In verse 9, Peter follows the statement by saying, "The Lord is not slack concerning His promise [to return]."

The picture becomes clearer when we consider the writings in the Book of Barnabas. Even though Barnabas is not part of the Biblical canon, it was highly esteemed in the early church by the early church fathers. Barnabas writes in his epistle that at the end of 2,000 years, Jesus would return. Considering these facts, the meaning behind the payment of two denarii was to mark the 2,000 years allotted to the church to evangelize the world. This 2,000-year period is called the Last Days and was announced by Peter on the Day of Pentecost.

The commission to take care of sinful man was placed in the hands of the innkeeper and the inn. This command came with a prepayment and a promise for more when the Samaritan returned from his journey. He says to the innkeeper, "Whatever you spend, when I come again, I will repay you."

What a portrait to a church who has long awaited the Messiah. It is Jesus who said, "And behold, I am coming quickly, and My reward is with Me, to give to every one according to his work. I am the Alpha and the Omega, the Beginning and the End, the First and the Last" (Revelation 22:12, 13). He promised in Mark 9:41, "Whoever gives you a cup of water to drink in My name, because you belong to Christ, assuredly, I say to you, he will by no means lose his reward."

As Alpha and Omega, First and Last, He promises to complete what He has started.

As Alpha and Omega, First and Last, He promises to complete what He has started. He is literally giving the guarantee of His own name to the reward system of the saints who take care of sinful man. This reward is promised to those who take care of sinful man. Our mission and commission is to go to where half-dead people are and take them to the "inn" to be cared for until He comes.

The Parable of the Good Samaritan Decoded

And behold, a religious man stood up
and asked Him, saying,
"Teacher, what shall I do to inherit eternal life?"
He said to him,
"What is written in the Bible,
and how well do you understand it?"
He answered and said,

"'You shall love the Lord your God with all
your heart, with all your soul, with all your strength,
and with all your mind,'
and 'your neighbor as yourself.'"
And He said to him, "You have answered rightly;
do this and you will live."
But he, wanting to justify himself, said to Jesus,
"And who is my neighbor?"
Jesus answered and said: "Adam went down from
the Paradise of God to Satan's domain.
There Satan stripped him of his
clothing, caused him to sin, and departed, leaving Adam
spiritually dead and separated from God.
Moses came down that road.
And when he saw him,
he passed by on the other side because
the Law revealed sin but could not remove it.
Likewise, Aaron, of the Levitical priesthood, when he
arrived at the place, came and looked,
and passed by on the other side because
the animal sacrifices could not permanently
remove sin and restore Adam's race back to God.
Then Jesus came!
He came where he was,
because sinful man could not come to Him.
And when He saw him, He had compassion.
So He went to him and bandaged his spiritual wounds,
and poured in the Holy Spirit and His own blood to heal
and revive his dead spirit.
He placed man's sins on the cross

and established the church to care for him.
On the next day, when He departed,
He paid the ministers for
2,000 years of labor.
He commissioned the ministers by saying,
'Take care of him;
and whatever more you spend,
when I come again, I will repay you.'
So your neighbor is any sinner
who is in need of salvation.
Go now and save them!"

The Parable Decoded

"A certain Samaritan"	Samaritans (half Jew)—Jesus (God/man)
"... came where he was"	Jesus came where we were in our sins.
"... bandaged his wounds, pouring on oil and wine"	The giving of the Holy Spirit and the blood of Jesus
"... set him on his own animal"	The cross, symbolized by the Old Testament animal sacrifices
"... brought him to an inn and took care of him"	The church
"... when he departed"	The Ascension
"... he took out two denarii"	Two days' wages or prophetically 2,000 years
"... gave them to the innkeeper"	The ministry
"Take care of him"	The commission of the church
"... and whatever more you spend, when I come again ..."	The prophecy of His return
"I will repay you."	God will reward.

Questions for Discussion

1. What is the first Scriptural instance of oil and wine together?

2. What story is told prophetically in the Parable of the Good Samaritan?

3. Who is the *certain man* in this parable?

4. What does *Jericho* depict in this illlustration?

5. What does Moses have to do with the Parable of the Good Samaritan?

6. True or False: The Law of God can reveal and remove sin. Defend your answer.

7. What sets apart the heritage or bloodline of a Samaritan?

8. What is the significance of pouring in the oil and the wine?

9. In this parable, what does the animal typify?

10. What is the role of the church in the Parable of the Good Samaritan?

Remember the former things of old, for I am God,

and there is no other; I am God, and there is none like Me,

declaring the end from the beginning,

and from ancient times things that are not yet done,

saying, "My counsel shall stand, and I will do all My pleasure"

(Isaiah 46:9, 10).

4

Rapture Codes in the Hall of Faith

Hebrews 11 is an historical account of men and women who overcame great odds and, through faith, walked in the will of God in spite of adversity, torture, and many times even death.

The Hall of Faith

The walk with the heroes and heroines of the faith leaves us speechless as we survey the many years of sacrifice paid by God's champions. Their trail of blood, sweat and tears leads us to the land of victory. Many of their corpses became stepping stones for the next generation. Each of them seemed to have a grasp of the big picture—the eternal land of victory—and they embraced that place in their hearts. While living in temporary conditions of pain, battle and strain, each pressed on providing such a powerful legacy of faith that future generations would be inspired by their stories to keep on believing.

Although this inspirational tour heralds a victor's song in every line, it is not the only song ringing in the hall. Also embedded in the stories is the prophecy code. Hebrews 11 is more than a reflection of the past; it is a light to the future. Looking back in time, the voice of the prophet Isaiah calls us to corners of the room in the great hall to look deeper into the meaning of the Holy Writ. Isaiah whispers to our spirit, "declaring the end from the beginning, and from ancient times, things that are not yet done" (46:10). His words compel us to look deeper at the stories to find more than a trail of bloody footprints. If we are diligent, we will find a trail of gold that leads to the celestial city of our God.

Enoch Reveals the Rapture

> By faith Enoch was taken away so that he did not see death, "and was not found, because God had taken him"; for before he was taken he had this testimony, that he pleased God (Hebrews 11:5).

Not much is recorded in Scripture about Enoch, who lived in the ancient world at the beginning of the human race. However, through the writer Jude, who was the half-brother of Jesus, we are given a spiritual revelation. It is not clear where Jude got his information since he wrote more than 4,000 years after Enoch's rapture. He could have received the story from Jesus. If not, then like other writers of the Holy Scripture, the Holy Spirit would have revealed it to him. Read carefully as we survey the only other passage in Scripture about Enoch.

> Now Enoch, the seventh from Adam, prophesied about these men also, saying,
>
> *"Behold, the Lord comes with ten thousands of His saints,* to execute judgment on all, to convict all who are ungodly among them of all their ungodly deeds which they have committed in an ungodly way, and of all the harsh things which ungodly sinners have spoken against Him"* (Jude 14, 15, emphasis added).

Enoch prophesied that tens of thousands of saints will be with Christ when He returns to execute judgment. Obviously, Enoch is talking about the second coming of the Lord, because we know the rapture of the church precedes the Second Coming. Enoch doesn't have to write about the Rapture, because God's plan is to use his life as an illustration.

The Rapture is not a single event in history, but it is a pattern of events, meaning there is more than one rapture in Scripture. There is only one rapture of the church, but the church is not the only one caught away in the sky. Enoch is the first of many who will be caught away to be with the Lord.

It is important to note that Enoch is the seventh man from Adam. Seven represents completion. The seventh day represented the day of completion for the earth. The pattern of seven as God's number of completion is played out in Scripture in more than 500 verses and in multiple illustrations. Adam is a representative of the first man in the human race. Enoch, the seventh generation from Adam, is God's representative of the completion of the human race—the seventh man.

The pattern of seven as God's number of completion is played out in Scripture in more than 500 verses and in multiple illustrations.

This is an interesting story. Look closely, and we will discover why God chose to rapture Enoch. In Genesis 4:17, Cain named his first son Enoch (not the Enoch who was raptured). This was Cain's first son after his curse. Verse 16 tells us that Cain went out from the presence of the Lord. After he killed Abel, Adam and Eve had their third son, Seth. Verse 25 tells us God appointed them another seed instead of Abel. *Seth* means "substitute." This scripture also states that Seth's line was appointed. Seth's family becomes the lineage of Abraham, which is in the lineage of Jesus Christ.

Let's trace the lineage and the significance of their names.

Cain, which means "to provoke," bears a son named *Enoch*, which means "to initiate or to teach." Enoch bears a son named *Irad*, meaning "fugitive." Irad has a son named *Mehujael*, which means "smitten of God." He had a son named *Methushael*, which comes from two words: *Meth*, where we get our word *math*, and *jael*, which is short for *Jehovah God*. His name literally translated is "math of God."

The next son is the seventh born of Adam in Cain's line. His name is *Lamech*, who is the *second murderer* in the human race. Genesis 4:24 says that if God avenged Cain sevenfold for his crime, then Lamech would be avenged "seventy-sevenfold."

Seth had a son whom he named *Enosh*, which means "man." Verse 26 says his birth was the beginning of prayer. Enosh has a son named *Cainan*, which means "to build a home or a nest." His son is *Mahalaleel*, meaning "praise of God." He had a son named *Jared*, meaning "to cast down the enemy." Jared is the father of *Enoch*, which we know means "to initiate or to teach."

Enoch had a son named *Methuselah*, which consists of two words: *meth*, translating "math," and *shelach*, which means "to leave or go away." Methuselah was the eighth generation signifying a new beginning. His name literally translates "the math of when things will go away."

If the name *Enoch* means "to teach," what is God trying to teach us through the life of Enoch?

◐ Enoch was the seventh man from Adam, representing the completion of man. He not only represents the last generation, he also represents the righteous. His rapture was not a mere coincidence. Rather, it was God telling the story of the redeemed from the beginning of time.

◐ At age 65, Enoch had a son named Methuselah, and Enoch lived exactly 365 more years. Methuselah is a son of prophecy. His days are numbered and the year of his death was the same year of the Great Flood which brought the destruction of mankind. Was it mere coincidence that Enoch named his son Methuselah and was then raptured 365 years after the prophecy began?

◐ *Methuselah*, which means "the math of when things will go away," was 187 years old when Lamech was born.

◐ Lamech was 182 years old when he had Noah.

◐ Noah was 600 years old when he entered the ark. Do the math: 187 + 182 + 600 = 969 years.

The Flood came the year Methuselah died. Genesis 5:27 says, "So all the days of Methuselah were nine hundred and sixty-nine years; and he died."

The life of Enoch reveals the prophecy code concerning the end times. He tells of three major events:

- ◐ The Rapture
- ◐ The coming Judgment
- ◐ The Second Coming

Enoch lived out the rapture, Methuselah numbered the days of man, and then judgment came. Last but not least, Enoch left a final word of hope to all generations: "Behold, He comes with ten thousands of His saints."

Noah Reveals the Rapture

> By faith Noah, being divinely warned of things not yet seen, moved with godly fear, prepared an ark for the saving of his household, by which he condemned the world and became heir of the righteousness which is according to faith (Hebrews 11:7).

Genesis 6:13-22 documents the building specifications of the ark:

- ◐ It was made out of gopherwood.
- ◐ It was covered with pitch, inside and out.
- ◐ It was 300 cubits in length (450 feet), 50 cubits wide (75 feet) and 30 cubits tall (45 feet).
- ◐ It had one window that was set 1 cubit (18 inches) from the top.
- ◐ It had one door on the side.

God sent the animals to Noah. He sent two of every kind of unclean animal and seven of every kind of clean animal. Most Bible scholars believe the window extended all the way around the top of the ark to give ventilation and light. The ark also had three levels or decks.

The purpose of the ark was to keep the righteous safe during the time of judgment on the earth. The altar call of Noah lasted 120 years. That's how long it took Noah and his family to complete the project of building the ark. I am sure that people came from everywhere to see this family preparing a huge boat situated on dry land that was nowhere near a large body of water. Noah would preach his message of repentance and the people would leave mocking and doubting.

Two of the most obvious 120-year patterns would be the life of Moses and the number of people in the Upper Room on the Day of Pentecost.

Types and Shadows

When we break down the types and shadows in this text, we begin to see an obvious trail of prophecy carefully carved by the Master Architect to point us to a future event—the rapture of the church. Judgment is coming on the earth, so God provides an ark of safety for the righteous. The 120-year message of repentance preached by Noah follows a pattern of the number 120 throughout Scripture. Two of the most obvious 120-year patterns would be the life of Moses and the number of people in the Upper Room on the Day of Pentecost. In each case, the number *120* signifies a time of restructuring. The 120 pattern is always the end of an era and the beginning of something new. Such is the case of Noah's message.

Another word for *ark* is the modern word *coffin*. In many ways, the story of the Flood can be compared to a death, burial and resurrection. According to the writing of the apostle Paul, baptism is symbolic of being buried and resurrected with Christ. The baptism of the earth was God's way of purifying the sins of the human race through death, burial by water, and resurrection.

The ark had three levels, just like a human being has a body, soul and spirit. God chose to use the ark as a type of embodiment of the righteous generation in the same way we are patterned after the Father, Son and Holy Spirit. The pitch sealed the ark inside and out from the water. And the pitch was the seal of protection, much like the indwelling of the Holy Spirit seals us to the day of redemption (2 Corinthians 1:22; Ephesians 1:13, 14; 4:30).

The animals came in groups of two and seven—the unclean animals in groups of two and the clean in groups of seven. The number *two* represents the spiritual man, in particular Christ, the Second Adam. Throughout Scripture, there is a pattern of God choosing the second over the first.

The pattern started with Cain and Abel and continues throughout Scripture to remind us that Christ, the Second Adam, came so that our spirits could overcome our flesh. Therefore, the unclean animals needed purification. They came in twos, not just because of a mating pair, but because three or four would have more easily populated their species. The number *two* symbolized the need for the unclean to be purified. However, the clean, or edible, animals came in groups of seven.

The gathering of the animals into the ark was a supernatural event, much like the supernatural event of God gathering His people to be redeemed from impending judgments.

If the clean animals were for food, why not six or eight? No, it was much more than just a food supply. The number *seven* is not a mere coincidence—remember, it is God's number of completion, symbolizing the fact that the salvation of the clean was complete. The gathering of the animals into the ark was a supernatural event, much like the supernatural event of God gathering His people to be redeemed from impending judgments.

Genesis 7:4 tells us that God told Noah to go into the ark and wait seven days before the earth was refined by water. Why wait seven days until the waters began? Was this a miscalculation on the part of Noah? Not at all. The seven days foreshadow the days of completion before the judgment of God on the earth. Seven letters are sent to seven churches in Revelation describing seven dispensations of the church. The Book of Revelation itself is seven sets of seven symbols. These 49 events lead up to the 50th event, which is God's eternal reward for the righteous—the ultimate jubilee. The seven days of waiting even tell the story of the seven years of tribu-

The seven days foreshadow the days of completion before the judgment of God on the earth.

lation that precede the Day of the Lord, a promised Judgment Day to purify the earth of evil.

The door in the side of the ark was closed by God himself. Jesus compared Himself to a door when He proclaimed in John 10:9: "I am the door. If anyone enters by Me, he will be saved, and will go in and out and find pasture." The door into Noah's ark was the only way to be saved, just as Christ is the only door to salvation. This door also foreshadows another door seen by John on the isle of Patmos.

> After these things I looked, and behold, a door standing open in heaven. And the first voice which I heard was like a trumpet speaking with me, saying, "Come up here, and I will show you things which must take place after this" (Revelation 4:1).

This was the Rapture moment of the Book of Revelation. At the end of the church age, John saw an open door in heaven, entered it and, from heaven's grandstand, watched the unfolding of the Great Tribulation. The trumpet voice correlates with the prophecy of Paul that a trumpet, or the trump of God, would precede the call to the saints at the catching away.

The ark being lifted above the water is a type of rapture.

Once inside the ark, the days of tribulation began for the earth. Sinful mankind was doomed. At a time that all seemed hopeless, the words that changed this scenario sounded forth like a trumpet. Genesis 6:8 says, "But Noah found grace in the eyes of the Lord." All of a sudden, the ark began to lift in the waters. This was the first boat of its kind, and the sight alone must have been astounding. It didn't take Noah and his family long to realize they were safe from the tribulation that was taking place on the earth. The ark being lifted above the water is a type of rapture. The saints of God will be lifted above the Tribulation when the Rapture takes place. The ark and its inhabitants were saved from the judgment and destruction. Eight people were on board the ark, which is the number that represents a new beginning.

At the end of the days of storm (Genesis 8), Noah sent out two birds to determine the status of the water. The first was a raven—a scavenger, unclean by nature. It never returned to Noah. Scripture tells us that it flew back and forth until the waters dried up. This bird represents the Adamic nature of man.

Noah also sent out a dove. It returned with nothing, but it did come back. The first dove is a type of the Creation story of the Holy Spirit hovering over the waters (Genesis 1:1). It is a picture of the Holy Spirit in the first testament that came upon man, but did not indwell him. It is also indicative of the salvation of the spirit of man, which overcomes the sins of the flesh; therefore, where the raven failed, the dove brought hope.

The second time the dove was sent out, she returned with an olive leaf in her mouth. The olive tree is certainly not the tallest foliage, so I'm sure there were other trees out of the water cover, as well. However, it was God's plan for the dove to bring the olive leaf. The olive tree speaks of Israel and God's promise to deliver His people. It also speaks of the olive oil used to anoint the priest and holy things. The first two times the dove was sent out are type and shadow of the Holy Spirit being poured out in the first and second testaments.

The apostle Paul also gives the olive tree as the symbol of Israel and tells the church that we have been engrafted into this branch.

Zechariah 4 speaks of two olive trees that pour oil into a lamp with seven stems of light. The trees give oil supernaturally without processing the olives by the hands of man, so basically, the lamp burns without being lit by the hands of man. The prophet asks what the vision means and is given these words: "[It's] not by might nor by power, but by My Spirit, says the Lord" (v. 6).

The apostle Paul also gives the olive tree as the symbol of Israel and tells the church that we have been engrafted into this branch. The return of the dove the second time with the olive branch represents the hope of Jesus as Messiah to restore Israel and make a way for the church to be engrafted into the branch of Israel. In the prophetic layer, it is the Holy Spirit's work in the Gentile church in the second testament. Therefore, the olive branch is a symbol of the Gentile church, as well.

The dove was not sent out again for seven days, which speaks of the completed work of God on the earth with the Jewish people who rejected the Messiah. God promised Daniel that He would give them

The sending of the dove represents the salvation of mankind through the agent of the Holy Spirit. seven additional years at the end of the age of the Gentiles. The third time the dove was released is a shadow of the outpouring of the Holy Spirit. Three flights shadow the third day and gives us the hope of the Messiah. So, it was in the third time the dove was sent—three being symbolic of divine completion—that the message became clear: *all is well.* In the prophetic layer, Christ was risen, and the Holy Spirit had been given to the church and was poured out on all flesh.

The sending of the dove represents the salvation of mankind through the agent of the Holy Spirit. We can't even know God unless the Spirit draws us. And after He draws us, He indwells us. The apostle Paul declares in Romans 8:11, "But if the Spirit of Him who raised Jesus from the dead dwells in you, He who raised Christ from the dead will also give life to your mortal bodies through His Spirit who dwells in you."

Once the ark that lifted them above the judgment had settled on the earth again, Noah and his family returned to the earth to rebuild it. This, too, is a portrait of the Second Coming, when Christ and the saints return to the earth to rule and reign for 1,000 years. The 1,000-year reign will be the fulfillment of the Feast of Tabernacles: God with us.

After the Flood, God showed us His physical presence on the earth in the form of the world's first rainbow. Until that time, the only rainbow that had existed was one that encircled God's throne. The bow in the sky was a half circle. It is almost as if God was saying, "This is My promise—you get half of the rainbow and I'll keep the other half as a sign of covenant."

Together, the two halves make a whole, and in the end, there is only one body, one tree, one Kingdom—just as there is only one Lord. The journey of Israel and the church are two separate roads that lead to the same place. In the end, every knee will bow to Jesus and every tongue will confess that Jesus is Lord.

Questions for Discussion

1. What New Testament chapter is considered the *Hall of Faith*? Why?

2. What marks the trail to the place of victory?

3. What words of Isaiah drive us to a deeper examination of Scripture?

4. What three future events are revealed in the life of Enoch?

5. Which New Testament writer gives us revelation concerning Enoch?

6. Enoch prophesied concerning what great event?

7. How does the literal translation of the names of Bible characters provide understanding of the broader picture of Scripture?

8. What part does mathematics play in discovering the prophetic layer in the story of Enoch?

9. Discuss the various types and shadows in the story of Noah.

10. What does the closing of the door of Noah's ark signify?

It is sown a natural body, it is raised a spiritual body.

There is a natural body, and there is a spiritual body.

And so it is written,

"The first man Adam became a living being."

The last Adam became a life-giving spirit.

However, the spiritual is not first, but the natural,

and afterward the spiritual.

The first man was of the earth,

made of dust; the second Man is the Lord from heaven.

As was the man of dust,

so also are those who are made of dust;

and as is the heavenly Man,

so also are those who are heavenly.

And as we have borne the image of the man of dust,

we shall also bear the image of the heavenly Man

(1 Corinthians 15:44-49).

5

THE SECOND ADAM

The Scriptural concept of the Second Adam, or "last Adam" (1 Corinthians 15:44-49) has to do with the spiritual man and the natural man. Both are part of every person. This passage explains that the natural man is first and then the spiritual man. It goes on to tell us that the natural man comes from the ground and the spiritual man comes from heaven. To be complete, the spiritual man must be born within every person so that the natural man can be freed from the curse of sin that came when Adam and Eve sinned in the Garden of Eden.

Understanding the concept of the Second Adam unlocks a pattern that appears throughout the Bible. The pattern is identified by God's choice of second things over

Understanding the concept of the Second Adam unlocks a pattern that appears throughout the Bible.

first things. While every pattern will not be articulated, a closer review of the prophetic layer of Scripture will show that in each of these incidences, the second choice becomes a *type* of Christ in the story. If we search the layers of types and shadows in the story, we will see the story of Jesus in living color, played out in the "second-choice" characters.

Here are a few of the second-choice patterns that can be easily identified:

1. Cain (natural man) and Abel (spiritual man)

2. Aaron and Moses

3. Ishmael and Isaac

4. Leah and Rebeccah

5. Esau and Jacob

6. Manasseh and Ephraim

7. Older brother and the Prodigal Son

8. Parable of the wedding feast—first group of guests and second group of guests

9. Day of Pentecost—the beginning of the second harvest (the barley harvest and the wheat harvest)

10. First Adam and Second Adam (Jesus)

THE NATURAL MAN AND THE SPIRITUAL MAN

Then to Adam He said, "Because you have heeded the voice of your wife, and have eaten from

the tree of which I commanded you, saying, 'You
shall not eat of it': Cursed is the ground for your
sake; in toil you shall eat of it all the days of your
life. Both thorns and thistles it shall bring forth
for you, and you shall eat the herb of the field. In
the sweat of your face you shall eat bread till you
return to the ground, for out of it you were taken;
for dust you are, and to dust you shall return"
(Genesis 3:17-19).

The ground is cursed because it is the substance
from which man was taken. God didn't have to curse
the ground. He could have just cursed Adam. By
cursing the ground, God instituted the curse at its origin that will continue to all future generations. In the
Parable of the Sower, Jesus identified the ground as
the world. In other words, it represents the human
race. From an exegetical point of view, the cursed
ground in the story of Adam is simply a curse on his
Garden, representing a punishment of toil and sweat.
However, from the prophetic layer of Scripture, we
can see that it has a deeper spiritual meaning: it represents the curse on the human race.

Cain and Able

Our narrative picks up in Genesis 4, with the birth
of Adam and Eve's first two sons: Cain and his
younger brother, Abel.

Now Adam knew Eve his wife, and she conceived and bore Cain, and said, "I have acquired
a man from the Lord." Then she bore again, this

time his brother Abel. Now Abel was a keeper of
sheep, but Cain was a tiller of the ground. And
in the process of time it came to pass that Cain
brought an offering of the fruit of the ground to
the Lord. Abel also brought of the firstborn of his
flock and of their fat. And the Lord respected
Abel and his offering, but He did not respect
Cain and his offering. And Cain was very angry,
and his countenance fell (vv. 1-5).

The two sons were born under the curse. The story
does not identify Cain as the natural man and Abel as
the spiritual man right away. Not until the key is given
in 1 Corinthians 15 is the prophecy code of the Second
Adam unlocked. However, with spiritual eyes, we
begin to see how the story of these two brothers tells
the story of Jesus and His saving blood.

In the Process of Time

In verse 3, the phrase "in the process of time"
shows Cain and Abel as grown-ups. They were not
little boys running and playing in the fields. Another
important part of this scripture cannot be ignored.
When Abel brought his offering to the Lord, he separated the fat, just as God would instruct Moses later
to designate the part that belonged to the Lord, or the
tithe. The inference is that Cain and Abel understood
the principles of presenting an offering to the Lord.

Cain's offering was described as "an offering of the
fruit of the ground." The description of Abel's offering
is that he brought a "firstborn" lamb and separated

the fat. The difference in these two offerings is obvious; one is a tithe offering and the other is not. If Cain's offering had been of the firstfruits of his field, the outcome would have been different.

Cain became angry because his offering was rejected, even though he had not heeded God's instructions. Cain was thinking with his head, while Abel walked in obedience because he feared the Lord in his heart. Cain could have also offered a lamb, because this first family shared everything—Abel ate the fruit Cain grew and Cain ate the lamb Abel tended.

Satan's plan was to destroy the spiritual man by convincing the natural man that the natural can get along without the spiritual. First Corinthians 2:14 reads: "But the natural man does not receive the things of the Spirit of God, for they are foolishness to him; nor can he know them, because they are spiritually discerned."

Satan's plan was to destroy the spiritual man by convincing the natural man that the natural can get along without the spiritual.

Satan convinces people today that spirituality is foolish. He wants us to feel our fleshly desires and allow our carnal man to control our lives. If the natural man prevails, the spiritual man will submit. If the spiritual man prevails, the natural man will submit. While mankind's existence is a dichotomy, the spiritual man must be stronger because the ways of the flesh are enmity against God.

Satan's Open Door

> So the Lord said to Cain, "Why are you angry?
> And why has your countenance fallen? If you
> do well, will you not be accepted? And if you
> do not do well, sin lies at the door. And its
> desire is for you, but you should rule over it"
> (Genesis 4:6, 7).

Cain understands that only obedience can cause him to be accepted. Among the strongest traits of natural man are pride and stubbornness. Cain's pride and self-centeredness will not allow him to submit to God's plan and bring an accepted offering. At the core of all sin is self-centeredness. Humanism is about seeing humans as the ultimate progression of the evolutionary process. Humanists believe humans are the ultimate being, thus self-worship is practiced as the only acceptable form of spirituality. Cain was warned that if he chose to obey God, he would be accepted, but if he chose to serve himself, sin was waiting to aid him in self-worship.

Killing the Spiritual Man

Instead of submitting to God's plan, Cain—the natural man—decided to kill Abel, the spiritual man. Satan was now controlling Cain's mind. The "sin lying at the door" had been conceived in his heart. This man who would not slay a lamb, slew his brother. Cain had no reason to kill Abel, but Satan did. Cain's issue was with God, not Abel. However, Satan's issue is with the spiritual man. He wants to kill the hope of reconciliation with God.

An interesting observation is that the first battle of man was lost in a garden—Eden—and the Second Adam won the first round of our victory in a garden called Gethsemane. The battle fought by the Second Adam was not a physical one—it was a spiritual battle. Only prayer, supplication and obedience to God prevailed over the temptation of His soul. God said to Cain, "What have you done? The voice of your brother's blood cries out to Me from the ground" (Genesis 4:10).

The battle fought by the Second Adam was not a physical one—it was a spiritual battle.

If we read this sentence only from an exegetical viewpoint, we miss the prophetic story. How is it possible for Abel's blood to speak? Remember, the ground was cursed. It was the original substance of man. Part of the curse was that when the body dies, it returns back to dust. As the spiritual man's body dies, the life in his blood enters the dirt from whence he came. As the blood of Abel fell, it caused the cursed thing to live. The life in his blood cried out to God.

Allow me to summarize. In the Old Testament, the human race was cursed with the sin of Adam. The only way mankind could be reconciled to God was through the animal sacrifices given to the priests under the law of Moses. Man hopelessly struggled to obey in the hope that he could conquer his flesh and carnal nature. But not even one man lived a sinless life. All have sinned and come short of the glory of God (Romans 3:23).

In the New Testament, God sent the Second Adam, who is Jesus the Christ. He took on the battle of man. He overcame temptation (the things of the world), crucified the carnal nature of man and freed mankind of sin. In the Garden of Gethsemane, He fought a spiritual battle of the mind to the point of exhaustion, and the next day He was sentenced to death by the courts of carnal men.

The spirit of Cain and Satan nailed Him to a cross in hopes of killing the plan of redemption. Jesus was laid in the earth, buried just like Abel. During these three days, He went into the heart of the earth to set the captives free. On the third day, He rose triumphantly over death, hell and the grave. He ascended into heaven and the Holy Spirit came to dwell in the lives of believers. The indwelling of the Holy Spirit gave our spirit life and freed us from the curse of self-worship. Now the spiritual man controls the carnal man for the first time since the fall of Adam and Eve in the Garden.

Genesis 4:12 tells us that the ground no longer yielded fruit to Cain. Cain was working the ground until the blood cried out; sin was working mankind until the blood of Jesus cried out. Before the Blood, Cain, our carnal nature, was working in us. We are that field, and Satan was having a "field day" with our lives. We had no choice because we were cursed. No matter how hard we tried, we always produced thorns and thistles. *Satan was working us.* But since the Blood fell on us, we no longer yield to him. We have been delivered!

The thing that used to bind us no longer has a hold because of the blood of Jesus. Just as an attorney pleads a case before a judge, Jesus pleads our case. The Blood does not lie—it tells the true story.

Just as an attorney pleads a case before a judge, Jesus pleads our case.

Christ's pure and sinless blood was shed for us. Our carnal nature is revealed. We thought we were princes, but now we can see that without Christ, we are fugitives and vagabonds. When Satan comes against the Blood, he realizes the new life created in us through Christ has conquered the curse.

The Second Eve

The first Adam chose a bride that was formed out of his side. She became the mother of all living things. Through her, new life entered the human race. But after she sinned, all she could produce was a sinful race.

The Second Adam, Jesus, also took a bride. Ephesians 5 tells us a mystery that was decoded by the apostle Paul. He tells us that a man should love his wife and a wife should obey her husband. After his poignant teaching on marriage, Paul reveals that he is actually speaking about Christ and the church. The marriage unit is a tangible illustration of Christ and His church.

John 19:34 tells us as Christ hung on the cross, a soldier pierced His side after He was dead. Blood and water flowed out when He was pierced. Once again, with a prophetic eye, we can see the story of the Second Adam correlating with the story of the first Adam. When the first Adam fell into a deep sleep, God brought his wife from his side. The Second Adam was half-dead. He was physically dead, but spiritually alive. At this moment His side was opened to reveal a birth canal that issued blood and water, the natural elements of birth.

Christ's death on the cross birthed His bride, the church.

Christ's death on the cross birthed His bride, the church. He said in Matthew 16:18, "I will build My church, and the gates of Hades shall not prevail against it." The church is the birthing station for new life in Christ, just as Eve was the mother of all living things.

Questions for Discussion

1. What is the Scriptural concept of the Second Adam?

2. What pattern is revealed by the concept of the Second Adam?

3. What type is illustrated by *second choice* in Scripture?

4. Cite a few of the second-choice patterns in Scripture. Discuss their relevance.

5. Where in Scripture do we find the decoder key for understanding the deeper revelation of the story of Cain and Abel?

6. How does Satan attempt to destroy the spiritual man?

7. What is at the core of all sin?

8. What gives voice to Abel's blood?

9. Why are we able to plead the blood of Christ and be victorious?

10. Identify the second Eve.

Then it came to pass on the third day, in the morning,

that there were thunderings and lightnings,

and a thick cloud on the mountain;

and the sound of the trumpet was very loud,

so that all the people who were in the camp trembled.

And Moses brought the people out of the camp to meet with God,

and they stood at the foot of the mountain. Now Mount Sinai

was completely in smoke,

because the Lord descended upon it in fire.

Its smoke ascended like the smoke of a furnace,

and the whole mountain quaked greatly.

And when the blast of the trumpet sounded long

and became louder and louder, Moses spoke,

and God answered him by voice. Then the Lord

came down upon Mount Sinai, on the top of the mountain.

And the Lord called Moses to the top of the mountain,

and Moses went up

(Exodus 19:16-20).

6

The Holy Spirit and the Prophecy Code

The "law of first mention" is a principle of interpretation that requires a careful review of the way God introduces new things. The first time something occurs in Scripture, God outlines principles and concepts that explain parts of the subject we can only understand by looking at its foundation. In order to better understand the Feast of Weeks, which is one of the primary focuses of this chapter, it is important to review the foundation God laid for this feast.

The Setting of the First Feasts

The feasts of Israel were set up as holy rehearsals for the children of Israel. Only later in history would Biblical scholars be able to explain the spiritual meaning of these rehearsals. Many Jewish people today

...feasts not only celebrate the past, but point the way to future events concerning Christ.

only see the celebration of the feasts as a way of commemorating their past and telling the "old" story again to the next generation. However, the Holy Spirit has unveiled the mystery of the feast to the church, and now we understand that feasts not only celebrate the past, but point the way to future events concerning Christ.

The children of Israel, under the leadership of Moses, made their exodus from slavery in Egypt after 430 years of bondage. The Book of Exodus gives us the Biblical details surrounding the first ceremonial feast called *Passover*, which got its name because God sent the Angel of Death to slay all of the firstborn in the land of Egypt. The only families spared the death of their firstborn were those who had the blood of a spotless lamb in its first year painted on the doorpost. When the Angel of Death saw the blood, he would "pass over" the house.

Subsequently, another feast was initiated by events that took place on a mountain called *Sinai*. At first, the events on this mountain and the feast that was later called *The Feast of Weeks* do not seem to correlate, but as the two scenes unfold entirely, the clear picture comes into view. Later on in Scripture, God gives Moses a diagram of all the feasts that should be kept each year to celebrate antiquity and prophecy. The ceremonies of each feast become a passion play, dedicated to remembering the past, yet at the same time, they serve as a holy rehearsal for a future event.

MOUNT SINAI, THE FEAST OF WEEKS, AND THE DAY OF PENTECOST

How can an event on Mount Sinai, the Feast of Weeks, and the Day of Pentecost have anything in common? God told Moses that the Feast of Weeks would occur 50 days after the Feast of Passover. Fifty days after the original Passover, Moses and the children of Israel have the Mount Sinai experience. This is the initial experience that will foreshadow the Feast celebration that becomes a holy rehearsal.

What are they rehearsing? The word *pentecost* means *fifty*. The Day of Pentecost is 50 days after the Feast of Passover. The Upper Room experience on the Day of Pentecost happens on the feast day known as the Feast of Weeks. If each feast is a rehearsal, then at some point and time in history, there will be a main event, completing the rehearsals. The Day of Pentecost is that event.

In order to understand the Mount Sinai experience, we need to break down the separate events that took place on the mountain of God. Each event is significant, because each foreshadows a future event that we now know as the Day of Pentecost. In order to see the direct correlation, it is necessary to see each part of the event separately. These are the events of the meeting with God on the holy mountain.

Moses' Ascension to the Mountain

The first event was Moses entering the mountain (see Exodus 19). As the people watched Moses ascend to the mountain, they began to fear that he would never return. Moses became consumed in the cloud of God that haloed the mountaintop. The people waited for days, but the old prophet still didn't come back. After 40 days of waiting, they assumed he was dead and turned to idol worship for comfort.

This part of the event could easily be likened to a type of rapture, since we have an ascension and a voice like a trumpet calling him upward. However, the character of Moses is not a type of the church—he is a type and shadow of Christ. From his bulrush basket, Hebrew/Egyptian upbringing, shepherd occupation, miracles, and ministry of deliverance, Moses depicts the Savior in many ways. Theologians commonly refer to him as a type of Christ. As such, we cannot view his ascension to the mountain as a type of rapture, but rather it is best compared to the ascension of Christ.

A Supernatural Manifestation

The presence of God was evidenced by the sound of a trumpet, by thunder, lightning, thick clouds, fire and a majestic voice. The result was trembling and quaking by the Israelites. Exodus 19:16-19 gives the details of the awe-filled sight. Sometimes when we reflect on moments where God showed up, we automatically think of angels fluttering, blue skies, soft cool breezes and nature's song. However, that is usually not the case. The scene on the mountain was so supernatural the people were terrified to look on God.

The same thing is true of an event we now call the Day of Pentecost. While we often think of it as an enraptured moment of joy, it was most likely a terrifying experience at first.

This came after a long, exhausting prayer meeting that lasted for days.

On the Day of Pentecost, after Jesus the Mediator had entered heaven, the mountain of God—Mount Zion (see Hebrews 12:22-29)—there were great manifestations of a supernatural presence in the Upper Room.

◊ A visible evidence of fire on people's heads

◊ The sound of tornado-type winds blowing through an enclosed building

◊ Strange languages and ecstatic utterances of 120 people

The supernatural is always unnatural because it supersedes all the parameters we know as acceptable and common. When the supernatural is at work, it can be exciting from an anticipatory view, but it is also so unpredictable, it can be frightening. Those who are deeply spiritual and trusting of the Lord are initial acceptors of such an event, while many others remain skeptical and some even fearful.

The Law Given

Exodus 19:16-20 and Deuteronomy 4 and 5 record that on the 50th day on Mount Sinai, the Lord wrote with His finger on the two tablets of stone. We refer to this divine inscription as the Ten Commandments. When Moses returned with these heavenly mandates, the people were involved in the act of idolatry. The only reason the Bible gives for their choosing idolatry is they thought Moses was not going to return.

The appeal of idolatry is that it offers instant gratification; therefore, no faith is required. Instead of approaching God with faith, people can clutch a wooden doll in their hand and call it their god, or gaze upon a large stone statue enshrined with shiny accessories and become emotionally deceived. Many today have chosen the same route of idolatry, having been convinced that the imminent return of our Lord has been delayed or canceled.

Seeing the people involved in idolatry, Moses broke the tablets of stone, the earth opened, and 3,000 people were slain. Moses went again to the mountain and God took His finger and wrote them again. When Moses came off the mountain the second time, his face was so aglow with the glory of God he had to veil it to hide the glory.

In the Upper Room, God wrote the Law by the Spirit, not on tablets of stone, but in tablets of the heart and mind (see Hebrews 8:10). The breaking of the old law brought the death of 3,000 souls; the giving of the new covenant brought life and 3,000 people accepted Christ and were filled with the Spirit as Peter preached in the streets of Jerusalem on the Day of Pentecost.

In the Upper Room, God wrote the Law by the Spirit, not on tablets of stone, but in tablets of the heart and mind (see Hebrews 8:10).

The Book of the Covenant

The Book of the Covenant was the civil law of the people. Each sin was atoned by the sprinkling of a blood sacrifice. The book was kept alongside the ark of the covenant was used by the priest in judging the people.

We commonly divide our Bible into two parts, calling one the Old Testament and the other the New Testament. While we won't argue with tradition and history, we must realize that the Bible is not two divisions, but rather one book. Since the writings of the New Testament are now almost 2,000 years old, they most certainly are not new. However, the writings of what we call the New Testament are indeed the explanation of the new covenant of Christ. He introduced the new covenant at the Last Supper as He took the cup in His hand.

Since that time, the new covenant became the law that governs Christian living for those who are indwelt by the Holy Spirit. Hebrews 8:1-6 declares that we now have a better Mediator, a better ministry, a better covenant—established on better promises.

The Tabernacle and Priestly Order

At Mount Sinai, God established the religious order of the Jewish people. He gave them priests, a Tabernacle, a system of ordinances or sacraments, the Sabbath as a day of worship and rest, and the holy feasts.

Hebrews 8:1-6 declares that we now have a better Mediator, a better ministry, a better covenant—established on better promises.

In the New Testament, the coming of the Holy Spirit established a new order. Now the tabernacle of God is in man. We have the priesthood of all believers, spiritual sacrifices offered in the spirit house, and life and ministry of Christ fulfilling the feasts of the Lord.

The Fiftieth Day

The Jews celebrate the Feast of Weeks 50 days after the Passover. The departure from Egypt to the coming to Mount Sinai was 45 days; for they came out on the 15th day of the first month. On the second day of this third month, Moses went up into the mountain. The people were given three days to purify themselves. This takes us to the fourth day of the third month, or the 49th after departing Egypt. On the next day, which was the 50th from the celebration of the Passover, the glory of God appeared on the mountain. This is the day that will mark the beginning of the first Feast of Weeks, or 50th day after Passover. The number 50 is symbolic of a jubilee, thus marking the Day of Pentecost as a spiritual jubilee.

The Voice of the Lord in the Mouth of a Man

When Moses came down from the mountain, he spoke with the voice of the Lord. The written word in the hands of the people also became the spoken word in the mouths of the people. Moses is the author of the five books of the Law, the Torah. Before this time, mankind had no written word. Later on, Biblical manuscripts would be discovered called the Book of Job that predate the books of Moses.

On the Day of Pentecost, a supernatural phenomenon happened that left the people of Jerusalem astounded. The voice of the Lord was once again heard in the mouths of God's people. When the Holy Spirit sat on those in the Upper Room prayer meeting, they began to speak in other tongues as the Spirit gave them the utterance to do so. Many of them spoke in the languages of the surrounding regions. As they spread into the streets, the people heard them speaking the mighty works of God in various languages.

This experience began to occur in other regions as the power of the Holy Spirit fell upon God's people. Since this was primarily a Jewish group, it was doubtful that the Gentiles could receive this supernatural imparta-tion. However, an Italian by the name of Cornelius, removed all doubt. He and his family had the same experience as did many other Gentiles when the Holy Spirit began to sweep throughout the land. When Peter returned to the Jerusalem Council to give a report of the growth of the Gentile church, his defense for their true conversion was, "They spoke in tongues just as we did."

THE MYSTERY UNVEILED

The word *mystery* is used many times throughout the New Testament to describe the unveiling of a deeper spiritual meaning. The appointed Feast of Weeks and the Day of Pentecost also unveil a mystery and prophetic truth.

The Feast of Weeks was held in the middle of the two harvests. The Holy Spirit was given in the middle of the life of Israel. The time of Abraham to Pentecost was approximately 2,000 years. The Holy Spirit came approximately 2,000 years ago. The purpose in cele-brating this feast was to celebrate God's provision for the harvest.

Prophetic Truth

The Holy Spirit is God's provision to reap the spir-itual harvest. The tabernacles set up by Moses repre-sented the temporary dwelling place of God. The

Holy Spirit now indwells a temporary temple, which is our body.
The Greek name for the Feast of
Weeks is *Pentecost*, meaning "fiftieth." The word is not used in the
Old Testament, but it is found
three times in the New Testament.

The Greek name for the Feast of Weeks is Pentecost, meaning "fiftieth."

The feast took place on the 50th day after the waving
of the sheaf of firstfruits (see Leviticus 23:15-16).

First Corinthians 15:20-23 says:

> But now Christ is risen from the dead, and has
> become the firstfruits of those who have fallen
> asleep. For since by man came death, by Man
> also came the resurrection of the dead. For as in
> Adam all die, even so in Christ all shall be made
> alive. But each one in his own order: Christ the
> firstfruits, afterward those who are Christ's at
> His coming.

Christ fulfilled the Feast of Firstfruits when He was
resurrected on the day of the feast. The Day of
Pentecost is 50 days later on the 50th day after Christ's
resurrection.

The Feast of Weeks

Several things had to be observed during the Feast of
Weeks. Each of these ordinances bring a greater significance to understanding the purpose of Pentecost. The
ordinances for this feast are given in Leviticus 23:15-21.

Israel never used leaven in their baking for a holy

feast. Leaven symbolized sin and thus was always left out. But the new meal offering required that leaven be left in the two loaves of bread that were offered to the Lord. Why was leaven found only in the meal offering at Pentecost and not in the meal offering at Passover?

The Passover symbolized Christ, who was without sin, thus leaven could not be used. Pentecost has to do with the church, made up of people who were born into sin and are not sinless. The two loaves represent the second grain harvest. The Feast of Weeks is the celebration of the end of the barley harvest and the beginning of the wheat harvest. In the Parable of the Wheat and the Tares, Christ reveals that the wheat represents the people of the Kingdom, or His church. The feast in the middle of the harvest is a picture of the outpouring of the Holy Spirit at the end of one harvest (Abrahamic Jews) and the beginning of a new one (the Christian church).

The Early and the Latter Rains

The two harvests depended on two rainy seasons, which became known as the early and latter rains. There can be no harvest without rains. The Lord promised Israel that He would bless her lands and send the early rains and the latter rains (see Deuteronomy 11:10-15; 28:12; Joel 2:23). The latter rain came during the time of the Feast of Weeks. The rain was to bless the new harvest and cause it to grow.

The spiritual significance of rain is a type of refreshing and revival (see Hosea 6:1-3). The prophecies of Joel tell us that God will pour out His Spirit in the latter days. The spiritual outpouring in the Upper Room was the spiritual fulfillment

The spiritual significance of rain is a type of refreshing and revival (see Hosea 6:1-3).

of the latter rains being poured out to reap the wheat harvest. The primary reason for the giving of the Holy Spirit was to fulfill the Great Commission. Jesus prophesied in Acts 1:8 the exact places where the revival would begin: "But you shall receive power when the Holy Spirit has come upon you; and you shall be witnesses to Me in Jerusalem, and in all Judea and Samaria, and to the end of the earth." It happened exactly as He prophesied.

The first rains fell in Jerusalem on the Day of Pentecost, reaping a great harvest of more than 8,000 souls in the first week. Next, it rained in Judea as the revival fires began to spread (see 2:13; 8:1). The next place we are told revival rains began to fall was in Samaria (Acts 8). Finally, the last part of the prophecy predicts a worldwide outpouring of the Holy Spirit, which is still going on today.

Bringing in the Sheaves

The people of Israel were told to come rejoicing as they brought in the sheaves of their harvest for an offering to the Lord (see Deuteronomy 16:16, 17; 28:47).

They were to come into His presence dancing with their offering in their hands. They would then distribute the offering to their sons, daughters, servants, strangers, fatherless, widows and the Levites. Joel prophesied about the outpouring of the Holy Spirit, when he said:

> "And it shall come to pass afterward that I will pour out My Spirit on all flesh; your sons and your daughters shall prophesy, your old men shall dream dreams, your young men shall see visions, and also on My menservants and on My maidservants I will pour out My Spirit in those days" (2:28, 29).

As Peter declared on the Day of Pentecost, "This is what was spoken by the prophet Joel" (Acts 2:16). He released a harvest of rejoicing into the hands of our sons and daughters, young and old, servants and strangers.

Feast of Weeks	Day of Pentecost
The Fiftieth Day	The Fiftieth Day
Writing of Ten Commandments on stone	Writing of commandments of love on tables of the heart and mind (Matthew 22:34-40; Romans 13:8-10).
Written by the finger of God	Written by the Spirit of God
Three thousand were slain—given death.	Three thousand were saved—given life.

Feast of Weeks	Day of Pentecost
The giving of the Law to guide a people	The giving of the Spirit to guide a people
Glory shone on the face of Moses.	Glory shone on the face of Jesus.
Moses' face was veiled so the people could not see the glory.	Veil was rent at Calvary to behold God's glory.
Mount Sinai	Mount Zion (Hebrews 12:22-24)
The Passover lamb offered	Jesus the Lamb of God offered
The meal offering at Passover—without leaven	The body of Jesus offered—without sin
The "new" meal offering at Pentecost—with leaven	The "new" body of Christ (church)—from the sinful man
The firstfruits offering in the middle of the harvest	The resurrection of Christ as our firstfruits
The celebration in the middle of the harvest	The giving of the Holy Spirit for the purpose of winning the harvest
The early and latter rains for the harvest	The outpouring of the Spirit for the harvest
The bringing of the offering—rejoicing into His presence	The rejoicing in the spirit which is shared to all who are in the wounded world

Questions for Discussion

1. What is the significance of the established feasts for the children of Israel?

2. What is commemorated by the first ceremonial feast?

3. Explain the correlation of Mount Sinai, the Feast of Weeks and the Day of Pentecost.

4. Discuss Moses as a type of Christ and the significance of His ascension on the mountain.

5. How was the presence of God manifested on the mountain, and what similarities are there to the manifestations on the Day of Pentecost?

6. Contrast the events of the giving of the Ten Commandments and the outcome with the Day of Pentecost and its immediate aftermath.

7. Compare the concepts of the Tabernacle and the priestly order between the Old and New Testaments.

8. What does the number *fifty* symbolize and what does it indicate with regard to Pentecost?

9. What is the purpose of celebrating the Feast of Weeks?

10. Examine and explain the spiritual significance of rain.

But Isaac spoke to Abraham his father and said, "My father!"
And he said, "Here I am, my son." Then he said,
"Look, the fire and the wood,
but where is the lamb for a burnt offering?"
And Abraham said,
"My son, God will provide for Himself the lamb
for a burnt offering." So the two of them went together.
Then they came to the place of which God had told him.
And Abraham built an altar there and placed the wood in order;
and he bound Isaac his son
and laid him on the altar, upon the wood.
And Abraham stretched out his hand
and took the knife to slay his son.
But the Angel of the Lord called to him from heaven and said,
"Abraham, Abraham!" So he said, "Here I am."
And He said, "Do not lay your hand on the lad,
or do anything to him; for now I know that you fear God,
since you have not withheld your son, your only son, from Me."
Then Abraham lifted his eyes and looked, and there behind him
was a ram caught in a thicket by its horns.
So Abraham went and took the ram, and offered it up
for a burnt offering instead of his son.
And Abraham called the name of the place,
The-Lord-Will-Provide; as it is said to this day,
"In the Mount of the Lord it shall be provided"
(Genesis 22:7-14).

7

THE LAMB OF GOD

The first mention of a lamb being offered to God was in Genesis when Abel offered a lamb in its first year to the Lord as a burnt offering. God's people continued to offer lambs as offerings to the Lord throughout Israel's history.

As we review the popular story of Abraham and Isaac going to the mountain, it is important that we view it through the lens of the prophetic layer of Scripture. The types and shadows of this story will beautifully overlay the story of Jesus dying on the cross.

The Lord Will Provide a Lamb

The story begins with Abraham's test of obedience to offer his only son, Isaac, as a sacrifice. Right away we can see the divine characters in the overlay. Abraham, the father, is offering his son, Isaac. John 3:16 declares that God gave His only begotten Son as a sacrificial love gift to the world. Isaac is the son of promise, as Jesus is the Heir of God. As they march up the side of the old mountain, many shadows come into view.

First we see Isaac's question, "Where is the lamb?" Abraham gives the prophetic answer, "God will provide the lamb." As Isaac begins to climb the hill, the wood is laid upon his back in the same manner that Jesus marched up Calvary's hill with the wooden cross on His back. The wood is laid on the altar and Isaac is bound to the wood. Jesus, in the same manner, was laid upon the wooden cross and bound to it with ropes and nails.

Isaac, being much younger and stronger than his aged father, had to submit to this act of being the sacrifice. Jesus also said, "Not my will, but thine, be done" (Luke 22:42, KJV). The Bible declares that the Angel of the Lord delivered Isaac, and stopped Abraham from sacrificing his son. The name *Angel of the Lord* is always capitalized in the Scripture, denoting it carries the title of Deity. This title is not referring to a particular angel, but rather a Christophany—or appearance of Christ in another age. While some debate this phenomenon, many scholars agree that the Angel of the Lord is Christ who manifests Himself in order to bring deliverance. Jesus said, "I have the power to lay down My life and raise it up again." Isaac is only a type, but the true Lamb gives life back to him. The ram in the thicket is God's announcement that a vicarious Lamb will be provided—a substitute. In the story of Abraham and Isaac, we begin to see the theme forming that God will provide a Lamb as the sacrificial offering for the sins of mankind.

THE BLOOD OF THE LAMB

Speak to all the congregation of Israel, saying: "On the tenth of this month every man shall take for himself a lamb, according to the house of his father, a lamb for a household. And if the household is too small for the lamb, let him and his neighbor next to his house take it according to the number of the persons; according to each man's need you shall make your count for the lamb. Your lamb shall be without blemish, a male of the first year. You may take it from the sheep or from the goats. Now you shall keep it until the fourteenth day of the same month. Then the whole assembly of the congregation of Israel shall kill it at twilight. And they shall take some of the blood and put it on the two door-posts and on the lintel of the houses where they eat it. Then they shall eat the flesh on that night; roasted in fire, with unleavened bread and with bitter herbs they shall eat it. Do not eat it raw, nor boiled at all with water, but roasted in fire—its head with its legs and its entrails. You shall let none of it remain until morning, and what remains of it until morning you shall burn with fire. And thus you shall eat it: with a belt on your waist, your sandals on your feet, and your staff in your hand. So you shall eat it in haste. It is the Lord's Passover. For I will pass through the land of Egypt on that night, and will strike all the firstborn in the land of Egypt, both man and beast; and against all the gods of Egypt I will execute judgment: I am the Lord. Now the blood shall be a sign for you on the houses where you are. And when I see the blood, I will pass over you; and the plague shall not be on you to destroy you when I strike the land of Egypt" (Exodus 12:3-13).

The choosing of the lamb was the beginning of Israel's deliverance. There were specifications. It had to be . . .

0   Without blemish in order to be offered

0   A male in its first year

0   Examined and separated from the flock for four days of cleansing and preparation.

Since Jesus died during the Feast of Unleavened Bread, it is easy to overlay the stories of the first Passover with the Seder meal referred to as the "Holy Supper" or "Last Supper." We can see the elements of Jesus' crucifixion in the broken bread and cup as He announced to His disciples, "This is My body and My blood." But what many people overlook are the events that preceded this meal.

The Triumphant Entry

Four days prior to the Feast of Passover, we have another story we often call the Triumphant Entry. It is a paradoxical story where the same people who hailed Him only days earlier are now crying, "Crucify Him!" A close examination of the story of the Triumphant Entry, along with the story of the first Passover, casts a clear shadow that connects the two events and gives understanding.

The choosing of the lamb included several instructions. First, the lamb had to be without blemish. Over and over, we see God requiring sacrifices without blemish. To be accepted, the red heifer had to be without one white hair. It had to be closely examined many times. The lamb also had to be reinspected for days to make sure there were no skin deficiencies. This is symbolic of the sinlessness of Christ.

Next, the lamb had to be a male in its first year. The firstlings were docile pets for Hebrew children. Their soft wool and playful nature made them ideal friends. This firstling represents the purity and innocence of Christ. Christ died on the cross as He was approaching His early manhood. At 33 years of age, He had not even entered the prime of His life. Even at 12 years of age, He was teaching the teachers in the synagogue.

God also told Moses that the sacrifice could be taken from the sheep or goat herd. It is interesting that our Lord instructs us later that God will separate the sheep from the goats on Judgment Day. The sheep represented the pure, innocent Lamb of God, while the goats symbolized the Adamic nature of man.

While the sheep solely represented Christ on the cross, the sacrificial scapegoat reminds us that we, too, were on the cross with Him.

Jesus was the God-man. He was born of humanity and Divinity. While the sheep solely represented Christ on the cross, the sacrificial scapegoat reminds us that we, too, were on the cross with Him. Our sins were nailed to the cross with Jesus because He was God's appointed substitute to die in our place.

The lamb was separated a total of four days for ritual cleansing and inspections. Is it mere coincidence that on the same day Jewish men were choosing their lambs for the Feast of Passover, Jesus rode a donkey through the streets of Jerusalem? While fathers were inspecting their flocks to find the one spotless lamb that would best please God's requirement, the Lamb of God was being hailed in the streets of Jerusalem. God's Lamb was being chosen and set apart at the same hour the lambs were being chosen, which were only symbolic types and shadows of the true Lamb. Four days later, the Lamb was sacrificed. From the time Jesus entered Jerusalem, it was four days until He was crucified. Their lambs were killed at a precise hour, ordered by God. The Lamb of God died at the exact hour the lambs were killed.

God's mandate was for the lambs to be killed at twilight (between 3 and 5 p.m.). They were instructed at the first Passover to take the blood of the lamb and put it on three places on the door. They were to smear it on the two doorposts and the lintel. That would display a bloodstain in four places in the doorway—the top, the two sides, and the bottom where the blood dripped down.

Jesus also had four distinct bloodstains on the cross—the top where the crown of thorns was, the two sides of the crossbar where His hands were nailed, and the bottom where His feet were nailed. If we overlay the cross in that doorway, the blood stains match perfectly. They had to eat the roasted flesh before morning. The lamb that is eaten is the same symbol given to us in holy Communion. The digestion of the bread in Communion and the lamb in Passover is the principle of salvation. To be our Savior, Christ must come into our life by choice. We have to invite Him in, much in the same way we choose to digest the bread and the lamb. The lamb had to be roasted with fire. This part of the passage is dif-

To be our Savior, Christ must come into our life by choice.

ficult for some to understand, until we realize that Jesus went into the heart of the earth, during those three days, to set the captives free.

The heart of the earth is called *upper Sheol*, or Abraham's bosom. It was a place of waiting until Christ came and unlocked the door to eternity. Now, to be absent in the body is to be present with the Lord (Matthew 12:40; Ephesians 4:8-10; 1 Peter 3:19-22; Acts 2:27-32). The blood on the door is what saved the family from the death angel at the first Passover. Jesus declares in John 10:7-9 that He is the door. Indeed, He is the doorway to heaven and the only way to God. We must all walk through that door and come under His sacrificial blood in order to be saved.

THE LAMB OF GOD

The next day John saw Jesus coming toward him, and said, "Behold! The Lamb of God who takes away the sin of the world! This is He of whom I said, 'After me comes a Man who is preferred before me, for He was before me.' I did not know Him; but that He should be revealed to Israel, therefore I came baptizing with water." And John bore witness, saying, "I saw the Spirit descending from heaven like a dove, and He remained upon Him. I did not know Him, but He who sent me to baptize with water said to me, 'Upon whom you see the Spirit descending, and remaining on Him, this is He who baptizes with the Holy Spirit.' And I have seen and testified that this is the Son of God" (John 1:29-34).

When John began baptizing the repentant people of Israel, he introduced to them a new concept. Self-immersion had been practiced for centuries as a ceremonial ritual for cleansing. However, John introduced two new concepts:

1. He baptized others by immersing them into the water after they had repented.

2. He announced that One would come after him who would baptize them with the Holy Spirit and with fire (Matthew 3:11).

Imagine the first crowd who heard that to be cleansed, someone was going to immerse them in fire. They couldn't grasp John's spiritual analogy at the time, yet they submitted to his new spiritual cleansing ritual. Prior to this, the act of baptism had only been performed by the priests for animals brought to be sacrificed. The reason for baptizing animals was to inspect them. God required these animals to be without spot or blemish. When a person brought a lamb to be sacrificed, the priest did this in order to examine the skin and establish whether or not the lamb was a worthy sacrifice. By dousing the lamb with water, the priest was able to look beneath the wool and see the condition of the skin and determine if the lamb had any skin discolorations or birthmarks. Any blemish seen by the priest voided that lamb from being sacrificed. Usually the lamb had already been inspected for several days by its owners before being brought to the priest.

Jesus was given the title "Lamb of God," as a testimony that He was not born with a natural human proclivity for sin. His supernatural virgin birth allowed Him to be born into the human race without the sins of Adam. A spot is a defiling mark that is picked up while walking imperfectly through life. Jesus was not only born a perfect sinless being, He also lived a perfect, sinless life.

The act of the baptism of Jesus was to establish a spiritual fulfillment of the requirements for all sacrificial lambs. This examination by

Jesus was not only born a perfect sinless being, He also lived a perfect, sinless life.

water was followed with an announcement from heaven that the Lamb was pure. He had no defect of any kind. Jesus prevailed upon John to fulfill the act of baptism as an offering of Himself to be examined by all who watched, that He was indeed without spot or blemish. The voice from heaven and the affirming presence of the Holy Spirit were proof to all that the Lamb was suitable, having no spot or blemish. God's Lamb was found to be without blemish before being offered.

The Annual Ritual

The sacrifice of a lamb as an offering for sin had been practiced for generations by the people of Israel. This annual ritual was performed by the head of the household who inspected his flock and selected a "family lamb." Once the lamb was selected, it would never leave the sight of the family. These lambs were carried everywhere the family had to journey, watched over with the greatest of care. The family would not take any chances that this lamb might pick up a spot and become unacceptable as a sacrifice.

When a lamb was chosen as the animal of sacrifice for a family, the father would fashion a nameplate that would be hung around the lamb's neck. The purpose of the nameplate was not as a precaution in case the family lamb was lost, but it served as an identity. When a lamb was accepted by the priest as a suitable sacrifice, the priest would call out the name of the family on the nameplate before he sacrificed the lamb on their behalf.

The introduction of Jesus as "The Lamb of God" by John was a declaration that Jesus was the family lamb of the Father, fulfilling all of the requirements of the sacrificial lamb. Jesus allowed Himself to be taken from among His disciples for the express purpose of being sacrificed.

Jesus had informed Peter that before the rooster crowed twice, Peter would deny Him three times. At the conclusion of Peter's third denial, the rooster crowed for the second time, and Jesus looked at Peter. Weeping bitter tears of guilt, Peter departed, knowing that the time of the second crowing of the rooster coincided with the exact time of day the previous day's sacrifice was removed, and the preparation of the current sacrifice was begun. When Peter looked at Jesus in that hour, he realized Christ was, in fact, the Lamb being prepared for sacrifice.

While Jesus hung on the cross, Pilate ordered the following superscription to be placed above His head: "Jesus of Nazareth, the King of the Jews." Written in Latin, Greek and Hebrew, the superscription was offensive to many of the Jews who were at the site of the Crucifixion. Jesus had already been mocked as a "King," but there is something here that is particularly Jewish which had to do with the revelation that Christ was the family lamb of God.

When writing the superscription in Greek or Latin, there was nothing that would reveal any hidden message concerning Jesus. However, when written in

Hebrew, a revelatory discovery is made. Hebrew letters are more than an alphabet to Jewish people. Each letter carries significant numeric value and also interpretive meaning. The first letter of each of the major words in a phrase was dropped down one space and capitalized, which means those four major letters in the phrase "Jesus of Nazareth, the King of the Jews" would be dropped down one space and capitalized. The Hebrew letters that were used in this fashion were YHWH. This was the reason for the anger of the Jews as they gazed at the superscription above the head of Christ.

The Hebrew letters that were used in this fashion were YHWH. This was the reason for the anger of the Jews as they gazed at the superscription above the head of Christ.

The Hebrew language has no vowels, and the four Hebrew letters YHWH form the name of God that Moses received when he asked God, "Who shall I say has sent me?" This is considered the most holy name of God by the Hebrews. In fact, it was thought to be so holy that it was unspeakable by human tongue, and they would not even dare to write it out. This was the nameplate of God the Father for His family which was being sacrificed for the sin of humanity. As was required, the family name identified whose lamb was being sacrificed. It was indeed the Lamb of God.

Questions for Discussion

1. Explain the prophetic layer of Abraham and Isaac.

2. Who is the Angel of the Lord?

3. Is there any correlation between the Passover Feast and the Triumphant Entry of Christ?

4. In this chapter, what represents the Adamic nature of man?

5. The sprinkling of the doorposts in the first Passover compares to _____.

6. What is a Christophany?

7. Prophetically, what does Isaac represent?

8. What is the prophetic significance of the sacrificial lamb having no blemish?

9. With regard to baptism, what two new concepts did John introduce?

10. Explain the significance of the nameplate. What was its importance in relation to Christ?

On the third day there was a wedding in Cana of Galilee,
and the mother of Jesus was there.
Now both Jesus and His disciples were invited to the wedding.
And when they ran out of wine, the mother of Jesus said to Him,
"They have no wine." Jesus said to her,
"Woman, what does your concern
have to do with Me? My hour has not yet come."
His mother said to the servants,
"Whatever He says to you, do it."
Now there were set there six waterpots of stone, according to the
manner of purification of the Jews, containing twenty or thirty
gallons apiece. Jesus said to them,
"Fill the waterpots with water."
And they filled them up to the brim. And He said to them,
"Draw some out now, and take it to the master of the feast."
And they took it. When the master of the feast
had tasted the water
that was made wine, and did not know where it came from
(but the servants who had drawn the water knew), the master
of the feast called the bridegroom. And he said to him,
"Every man at the beginning sets out the good wine,
and when the guests have well drunk, then the inferior.
You have kept the good wine until now!"
This beginning of signs Jesus did in Cana of Galilee,
and manifested His glory; and His disciples believed in Him
(John 2:1-11).

8

TURNING WATER INTO WINE

efore exploring the types and shadows in the first
miracle of Jesus, it is important to lay a good foundation for this spiritual analogy. To understand
water as a type of the Holy Spirit, we need to look into
some of the teachings of Christ where He used this
spiritual concept. In John 7:37, 38, Jesus says, "If anyone thirsts, let him come to Me and drink. He who
believes in Me, as the Scripture has said, out of his
heart will flow rivers of living water." Verse 39 explains
the saying by giving this interpretation: "But this He
spoke concerning the Spirit, whom those believing in
Him would receive; for the Holy Spirit was not yet
given, because Jesus was not yet glorified."

Water Is a Symbol of the Holy Spirit

Jesus was using the concept of water to describe a
spiritual truth about the Holy Spirit indwelling believers. The analogy insinuates that those who drink from

the living water Christ gives will be endued with a spiritual river that will continually flow out of their hearts and lives. The English word *heart* is translated from the Greek word *koilia*, which can be interpreted "belly, inner cavity or innermost being." The idea is that this river flows from our spirit and soul.

This was not a new concept. Isaiah 44:3, 4 says

"For I will pour water on him who is thirsty, and floods on the dry ground; I will pour My Spirit on your descendants, and My blessing on your offspring; they will spring up among the grass like willows by the watercourses."

The prophet spoke of the Holy Spirit being poured out—a prophecy Joel reiterates (2:28) when he prophesied that the Holy Spirit will be "poured out" on God's people.

The Setting of the Story

"On the third day there was a wedding in Cana of Galilee, and the mother of Jesus was there. Now both Jesus and His disciples were invited to the wedding" (John 2:1, 2). Note that the Holy Spirit who inspired John to write this Gospel impressed upon him to introduce this story as happening on the third day. Scholars have debated the meaning of stating this deliberate day for centuries. Some believe it was referring to the third day after He talked with Nathaniel, which is recorded in the first chapter of John.

Others have concluded that since a wedding celebration lasts for seven days, it was describing their arrival on the third day of the wedding gala. Regardless of the interpretation, it is certainly not the only time the third day is mentioned in Scripture. As a matter of fact, there is a third-day pattern that runs through the prophetic layer of Scripture.

In each occurrence of this pattern, the end result is always the same—a divine completion. Just as the number *seven* describes patterns of a completed act on earth, the third-day pattern always denotes that God is completing something spiritual.

Just as the number seven describes patterns of a completed act on earth, the third-day pattern always denotes that God is completing something spiritual.

The third day is mentioned almost 50 times in Scripture. A few of these patterns are easy to identify:

- ❶ Jonah was three days in the whale's belly.

- ❶ Jesus rose from the dead on the third day.

- ❶ God required three days of sanctification from the children of Israel before allowing them to go into the land of Canaan.

Another interesting fact in this story has to do with where this first miracle took place. Interestingly enough, Jesus begins and ends His ministry with a wedding. How appropriate since we are told in Ephesians that the love between a man and a woman is symbolic of Christ and the church. Jesus chose to launch His ministry at this wedding by performing His first miracle. He also made sure we knew the wedding was in Cana, which is the same root word for the land God gave to Abraham and is a type and shadow of the land of victory.

Since God does not waste words, He *wants* us to know that Mary was there also. The exegetical layer of this passage doesn't reveal anything significant about her presence, but a spiritual analogy of the scene shows otherwise. We have already demonstrated how water is a symbol of the Holy Spirit. When Nicodemus came to Jesus, he was told by the Lord that he must be born of the water and of the Spirit. Jesus wasn't referring to baptism, but rather a natural birth accompanied by the breaking of the water. That is why He reiterates the difference in the two births—one being of the flesh and the other being of the Spirit. The presence of Mary symbolizes both births. Since the mother of Jesus was Mary and His father was the Holy Spirit of God, His birth was a product of a water-and-Spirit birth. However, Jesus told Nicodemus that we all must be born again. We have already been born of the flesh, but now we must be born of the Spirit.

The Significance of the Wine

> And when they ran out of wine, the mother of Jesus said to Him, "They have no wine." Jesus said to her, "Woman, what does your concern have to do with Me? My hour has not yet come."

His mother said to the servants, "Whatever He says to you, do it" (John 2:3-5).

Let's put this into its spiritual context and see the significance of the wine at the wedding. First of all, the wedding symbolizes our marriage to Christ or our relationship to the Bridegroom. This, of course, speaks of our salvation experience when we accept Him as our Lord and Savior. We have been born of the water, our natural birth, and now that we have accepted Jesus, we have been born of the Spirit, our spiritual birth. This is symbolized by the fact that Mary was there and also by the fact that the disciples were present.

A closer look at the Parable of the Wedding Feast (Matthew 22:1-14) will also give insight to this analogy. The guests at the wedding feast are the people of the world who have been invited to come by the Lord of the house. Therefore, let us conclude that the guests at this wedding are symbolic of the *people* of the Kingdom; the disciples are symbolic of the *leaders* of the Kingdom; and Mary, the mother of Jesus, is the embodiment of the salvation experience of the two births necessary to enter into the "marriage" or relationship with Christ.

Now that we understand the characters of our story, how does this help us understand the purpose of the wine? We can only understand the spiritual analogy of wine if we listen to the words of Jesus at the Last Supper. He stated that the wine was His blood

and representative of a new covenant. On the Day of
Pentecost, those who were filled with the Holy Spirit
were accused of being intoxicated on new wine. The
concept of "new wine" is repeated in Scripture and
indicates a time of refreshing and newness of life. If
we understand the wine was a symbol of the old
blood covenant accompanied by the works of the
Holy Spirit in the first Testament, it will help us see
this picture more clearly.

The Holy Spirit is God's agent in dealing with
mankind in both Testaments. His presence always
accompanies anointings, outpourings, revivals and all
supernatural events where God uses a man to do a
supernatural thing. Let us conclude
that the wine in the John 2 passage
symbolizes the old covenant, which
depended on animal sacrifices and
the works of the Holy Spirit, in order
to bring any semblance of hope to
humanity that they are saved from
their sins.

The Holy Spirit is God's agent in dealing with mankind in both Testaments. His presence always accompanies anointings, outpourings, revivals and all supernatural events where God uses a man to do a supernatural thing.

This group, this Jewish group, has
run out of wine. Their rejection of the
Messiah caused them to walk
through life blindly with a veil over
their faces. The old blood covenant
and the old way the Holy Spirit
came upon a man for supernatural service was chang-
ing because of the Messiah's arrival on earth. "They"

ran out of wine. This is an expression about the Jewish people who were bound to their old covenant.

But then Mary, the mother of Jesus, approached Him and said, "They have no wine." If Mary was just an ordinary woman, why would she assume that Jesus would perform His first miracle at this particular place? But, she was no ordinary woman. She had a unique advantage over others in that she was a prepared vessel to house and raise the Son of God. Her body had carried the Holy Spirit for nine months in the form of a spiritual fetus. She was bonded to God through her natural, motherly bond to her son.

Mary was not ordinary in any sense of the word. From her angelic visitations to her late-night talks with her son, she was formatively spiritual in every way. She understood the deep things of God. There is no Biblical proof of her immaculate conception and assumption as many believe; however, we should not allow man's idolizing of this great woman to dim our view of her status. She was the mother of God on this earth. She was a chosen and prepared vessel of honor. Mary was key to the Messiah coming to earth, and again, this "prophetess" understood the deep things of the Lord. Her statement to her son was not ordinary. It was divinely inspired and was meant to be a spiritual conversation between the two.

Mary was key to the Messiah coming to earth, and again, this "prophetess" understood the deep things of the Lord.

Mary's implication that they needed more wine was a request to invoke the new covenant early. That is why Jesus' response was, "My hour has not yet come." He knew that the Holy Spirit would come and indwell every believer after His crucifixion, resurrection and ascension. However, Jesus chose to set the stage for it all by giving a spiritual illustration of things to come. When Jesus replied, "My hour has not yet come," Mary understood what her son was saying. Others in the room were confused at this strange conversation, but not Mary. She knew that her son, the Lord, was about to give them a spiritual illustration. Therefore, she said to the servants in the room, "Whatever He says to you, do it."

The Vessels

> Now there were set there six waterpots of stone, according to the manner of purification of the Jews, containing twenty or thirty gallons apiece. Jesus said to them, "Fill the waterpots with water." And they filled them up to the brim (John 2:6, 7).

Our God of precision made sure we understood the spiritual truth of this scene by giving us easy clues that unlock the prophecy code embedded in this passage. He began by making sure we, the readers, knew that there were six waterpots made of stone. *Six* is the number of man in the prophetic layer of Scripture. To begin with, man was created on the sixth day of Creation.

Another symbol of Christ, the menorah, has seven branches (one taller in the middle) filled with oil and a wick. A careful observation of this piece of furniture in the inner court of the Holy Place will reveal a precise plan of salvation through Jesus, the Light of the World. Even the way the menorah is lit explains the plan of salvation. The six branches made in the form of almond buds tell the story of mankind's journey to God. The almond bud is the first bud of spring, representing new life.

The almond bud was also the miracle that separated Aaron from the rest of Israel, calling him out as the high priest. The oil in the bud was a symbol of the Holy Spirit. The wick in the oil represented sinful man who needed new life (almond bud), the oil (Holy Spirit), and the true branch (taller middle branch of the menorah, Jesus), in order to have light (fire given from the taller branch).

Even the position of the taller branch tells how Christ was the bridge between two spiritual ages of mankind. The first was the spiritual age *prior* to the coming of Messiah, and the latter was the new covenant and spiritual age *after* His coming. The number *six* represents man, and we are told by John that there were six waterpots of stone representing all of mankind on the earth.

The waterpots were made of stone, which was hardened clay. They were not wooden or metal, but rather they were made from the material God originally chose to fashion mankind. These six earthen vessels are a symbol of man. The pots were evidently partially filled. There is a variance in how much water each of the six pots contained, but the Master instructed them to fill each pot to the brim. Filling them to the brim tells the spiritual story of the Holy Spirit filling up the vessel of man entirely. Instead of coming upon man for moments of spiritual conquest, Jesus was illustrating how we will be completely indwelt by the water, or presence, of the Holy Spirit.

John gave us another clue for unlocking the code when He said these pots were for the purification of the Jews. Indeed, the only way a Jewish person under the Law of Moses could be purified was through their partial understanding of Scriptures since their eyes had been veiled. Thus, the pots were not full. By filling the pots to the brim, Jesus illustrated that His new covenant would not be a partial cleansing or a ritualistic annual cleansing, but rather a saturated presence of the water filling every part of the vessel of man.

In the Parable of the Ten Virgins (Matthew 25:1-13), we are given another spiritual lesson that has often been misinterpreted. Many claim this is a differentiation between the serious Christians and the insincere ones. They claim the rapture of the church will be a partial rapture, taking only the sincere and "holy" ones while leaving all other believers behind. This parable *does* have to do with the church, but in no way does it insinuate the partial-rapture theory.

There are two groups in the parable, five in each group. *Five* is the number of grace in the prophetic layer of Scripture. The first group represents the Jewish people, and the second group represents the church. Both groups have the same lamps, which represent the Word of God. Both groups have the same oil in the lamps, which is the Holy Spirit. Both groups are looking for the same bridegroom,

Five is the number of grace in the prophetic layer of Scripture.

which is the Messiah. Both groups are waiting on the wedding feast. Both groups are asleep, not just the foolish virgins. Both groups are virgins.

The only difference in the two groups is more oil. The second group was under the new covenant of Christ and was indwelt by the Holy Spirit, defined by their having more oil. The first group was under the old covenant and received the first outpouring of the Holy Spirit but was never indwelt by Him, through their faith in Jesus Christ. The parable goes on to say, they would need to go out and get the extra oil at the same place the first group got theirs.

These six waterpots in John 2 give us the hope that the Holy Spirit wants to indwell any person who comes under the new covenant of Christ, thus totally purifying the Jews who accept Jesus as Messiah.

The Water and the Wine

> And He said to them, "Draw some out now, and take it to the master of the feast." And they took it. When the master of the feast had tasted the water that was made wine, and did not know where it came from (but the servants who had drawn the water knew), the master of the feast called the bridegroom. And he said to him, "Every man at the beginning sets out the good wine, and when the guests have well drunk, then the inferior. You have kept the good wine until now!" (John 2:8-10).

"Draw some out now, and take it to the master of the feast" was the instruction given to the servants. A twofold concept is introduced here. The first concept is an indication of the Rapture; the waterpots represent mankind. Obviously, all of mankind will not be taken in the Rapture. This drawn-out group is taken from the waterpots and presented to the master of the wedding feast. In the Parable of the Wedding Feast, the master is the bridegroom's father. If Jesus is the bridegroom (Mark 2:19, 20), the master of the wedding feast is His Father.

The presentation of the drawn-out ones is a type and shadow of the rapture of the church.

The presentation of the drawn-out ones is a type and shadow of the rapture of the church. It goes on to say that when the master of the feast tasted the wine, he did not know where it came from. What a beautiful portrait of grace. Our righteousness is as filthy rags and we have no hope within ourselves of making it to heaven in our own righteousness. However, the blood of Jesus purchased us, redeemed us, and now His righteousness covers us. "For He made Him who knew no sin to be sin for us, that we might become the righteousness of God in Him" (2 Corinthians 5:21).

The master of the feast accepted the converted water; he accepted it as wine, not knowing or caring where it came from. When we come to Christ, old things are passed away and behold all things become new. Our past is behind us, in Him. It doesn't matter how long it took us to get to Him; once we are converted, we are pure.

The second concept introduced here is the fact that inside the pots, it was still water, but when it was drawn out, it became wine. There is no indication that the water became wine in the pots. It is only wine as it is drawn out. This part of the drawn-out concept does not deal with our final state of rapture, but it has to do with the part that is given to the rest of the wedding guests. Ultimately, we will be presented to the Master of the wedding feast, but we will also be drawn out to

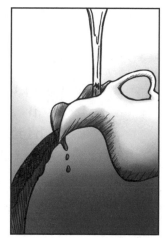

be presented to the wedding guests, who are the people of the earth. This concept has to do with being filled with the Holy Spirit. It is one thing for the water (the Holy Spirit) to be poured into the pots, but when it comes back out, it has been converted into a new substance—wine.

The wedding guest proclaimed that the former drink was inferior to the latter drink, and the best was saved for last. All believers are indwelt by the Holy Spirit at the time of their conversion. No man can even come to God unless the Spirit of God draws him.

We commonly say Christ is living in our heart. That is true from the standpoint that we have accepted Jesus as our Savior, but He is our Intercessor in heaven, seated at the right hand of the throne of God. The new presence we feel and experience is the indwelling of the Holy Spirit in our life. However, the *indwelling* of the Holy Spirit and the *infilling* of the Holy Spirit are separate events. One has to do with His coming in, the other has to do with His coming out.

The Parable of the Swept House tells us that we have to be occupied or the oppressors of our past will come back with more allies than before, and the latter state of that man will be worse than the former (see Matthew 12:43-45; Luke 11:24-26).

At salvation, the Holy Spirit occupies the vessel, but that does not mean He will overflow out of that life.

The pouring in of the water is the indwelling of the Holy Spirit, but the drawing out of the "new wine" is the outflow of the Holy Spirit that is commonly called *being filled* or *baptized* in the Holy Spirit. A spiritual transformation of boldness and power takes place when we allow the Holy Spirit to flow out of us to the other wedding guests.

The drawn-out water is now wine in the cup. As we yield ourselves to the person and works of the Holy Spirit, we will take on the transformed nature of wine. We will do the works of the new covenant by taking the blood of Christ to others. We will do the works by operating in spiritual gifts that may be interpreted as spiritual intoxication such as happened on the Day of Pentecost. That which flows out of our lives will not be of our own making, but rather will be a supernatural overflow of spiritual things as our vessels are yielded to the will of the Spirit.

The human body is made up mostly of water. The human spirit mirrors that fact as we are indwelt by the Holy Spirit. However, the water is given to occupy the vessel for cleansing purposes. But when it is drawn out, it becomes a tangible, tasteful power that is able to teach, transform and do the works of

Everything God has made, He proclaims to be good. He affirmed every day of His Creation with the acceptability phrase, "It is good."

Christ at a new level of spiritual boldness and spiritual sensitivity.

Everything God has made, He proclaims to be good. He affirmed every day of His Creation with the acceptability phrase, "It is good." The psalmist David declares, "Oh, taste and see that the Lord is good" (Psalm 34:8).

If we can spiritually taste the good things of God, it is therefore possible for the Lord to taste of our spiritual fruit as well. The master of the feast tastes the wine and declares it is good. Those who are baptized in the Holy Spirit become a sweet taste in the Master's palate. He affirms us by saying, we are good because we have allowed Him to transform us from water to wine, from carnal to spiritual, from a container to a cup. We are no longer seeking to fill ourselves or consume spiritual things for ourselves, but we become yielded vessels to be used by the Master for His guests, His feast, His honor, His glory, His purpose and His plan.

The master did not know where the water/wine came from, but the servants knew. One of the most

Every time we hear the Master say, "It is good," we can rejoice over our sinless life through Christ.

wonderful gifts of grace is that we can remember what God has chosen to forget. While we may not consider this a gift, it is a constant reminder of the goodness of God in our lives. Everyone has a testimony that no one has ever heard before. The deepest secrets of our thought life and private moments reveal a side of grace we can never share with anyone else.

Every time we hear the Master say, "It is good," we can rejoice over our sinless life through Christ. We worship Him out of those deep places that we remember. Each shameful memory reminds us of the depth of the love of God and the transforming power of the Holy Spirit. We can enthusiastically rejoice each time we remember where the water came from and how He turned it into wine.

Finally, the master declared, "You have kept the good wine until last." This is an expression of the better covenant. Hebrews 8:6-12, declares:

> But now He has obtained a more excellent ministry, inasmuch as He is also Mediator of a better covenant, which was established on better promises. For if that first covenant had been faultless, then no place would have been sought for a second. Because finding fault with them, He says: "Behold, the days are coming, says the Lord, when I will make a new covenant with the house of Israel and with the house of Judah— not according to the covenant that I made with their fathers in the day when I took them by the hand to lead them out of the land of Egypt; because they did not continue in My covenant, and I disregarded them, says the Lord. For this is the covenant that I will make with the house of Israel after those days, says the Lord: I will put My laws in their mind and write them on their hearts; and I will be their God, and they shall be My people. None of them shall teach his neighbor, and none his brother, saying, 'Know

the Lord,' for all shall know Me, from the least of them to the greatest of them. For I will be merciful to their unrighteousness, and their sins and their lawless deeds I will remember no more."

This is the promise of the new wine Jesus spoke of at the Last Supper—the new covenant of His redemptive blood and the giving of the Holy Spirit to indwell the believer. The first wine given at the feast was processed by the hands of man, like the keeping of the law processed and conditioned the heart of man. But the new wine was supernatural and spoke of a work that only God could do for mankind. First John 5:8 says, "And there are three that bear witness on earth: the Spirit, the water, and the blood; and these three agree as one." The Holy Spirit, the water and the blood (wine) are all used in this spiritual analogy to describe one eternal truth: God dwells in people whose bodies are the temple of the Holy Spirit.

Cups Running Over

Psalm 23 is often quoted at funerals for its comforting passages, but this is a prophetic psalm about the ministry of Jesus that speaks of a day . . .

- **◐** When the Good Shepherd will come and restore the souls of His people

- **◐** For conquering enemies, sleeping in pastures and walking in valleys without fear

- **◐** When God supplies the needs of His people

O When grace and mercy follow them around as protectors of their souls

O When we will dwell continually in the house of the Lord and our cup runs over.

One of the verses in this passage relates to our story at the wedding feast. It speaks of a day when our heads are anointed, and we are given a table even in the presence of our enemies. This can't be referring to the millennial reign of Christ because the Enemy is bound then. Neither can it refer to our eternal state because our souls will not need restoration; we will not know fear then, nor will we have valleys, any wants or enemies. It can only refer to a time when the Good Shepherd appears the first time on the earth and leaves us with the better covenant of turning water into wine.

This psalm gives us two particular promises that unlock the prophecy code. The first is the anointing of the head with oil, and the second is the overflowing cup. The first was only used when anointing kings and priests in the first testament of Scripture. The indication of our heads being anointed at the coming of the Good Shepherd indicates that we will enter our kingly and priestly reign in the spiritual sense of the Kingdom.

As a priesthood of all believers and as ones who can go into the Holy of Holies and boldly come before the Lord, we can understand our priestly title.

As a priesthood of all believers and as ones who can go into the Holy of Holies and boldly come before the Lord, we can understand our priestly title. And as ones having spiritual authority over demons and spiritual dominion of things of this earth, we also understand our kingly title. This is all part of the transformation in our lives when water becomes wine, or when we leave a state of intellectual and carnal existence and begin to flow in spiritual things.

The overflowing cup also speaks of being overfilled. The spilling over is the key that unlocks the prophetic code. This is a direct prophetic reference to a day when our vessels will spill over and overflow with a blessing so complete, we can give it away to others. The overflowing cups take place at the table that is spread in the presence of our enemies. This tells us that although we fight a spiritual battle on earth, the power of the Holy Spirit not only sustains us, but also gives us *more* than enough so that others can receive.

When the water is turned into wine, the Holy Spirit draws things out of us that we know we didn't generate or create. It is only in the outflow that the miracle takes place. Those who choose to hold tightly to their ticket to heaven will certainly make it, but those who allow themselves to be used for Kingdom work will take others with them. The overflowing cup of their life will allow others to drink at the wedding feast in the Master's house.

Questions for Discussion

1. Explain the meaning of the third-day pattern found throughout Scripture.

2. Approximately how many times is the third-day reference found in Scripture?

3. How does Jesus begin and end His ministry? Explain.

4. Explain the significance of Cana as the location of the wedding.

5. Explain the presence of Mary, the guests and the disciples at the wedding and what each represents.

6. What does the *new wine* represent?

7. Explain the prophetic implication of the six waterpots.

8. Prophetically, who is the "master of the wedding feast"?

9. What is the difference between *indwelling* of the Holy Spirit and *infilling* of the Holy Spirit?

10. In Psalm 23, what are the promises that help to unlock the prophecy code?

Then those who feared the Lord spoke to one another,

and the Lord listened and heard them;

so a book of remembrance was written before Him

for those who fear the Lord and who meditate on His name.

"They shall be Mine," says the Lord of hosts,

"on the day that I make them My jewels.

And I will spare them

as a man spares his own son who serves him."

Then you shall again discern

between the righteous and the wicked,

between one who serves God

and one who does not serve Him

(Malachi 3:16-18).

9

UNLOCKING THE RAPTURE CODES

The subject of the Rapture has sparked controversy for ages. There are those who believe in a pre-Tribulation Rapture, others who believe in a mid-Tribulation Rapture, and still others who believe in a post-Tribulation Rapture. Beyond that, there are even those who believe the whole concept of the Rapture is merely a spiritual metaphor.

Interestingly enough, many of them use the same scriptures to prove their points. Overall, they use their own paradigm and concept of the kingdom of God to persuade their school of thought. The heated debates rarely sway anyone from the other side. Inevitably, it is not possible for all Christians to agree on this subject, and perhaps we never will until after the event takes place.

I believe the Rapture is literal. I believe the Rapture

pattern has been established in many places throughout Scripture. The Rapture should not be viewed as a single event, but rather as a pattern of events. The patterns include the raptures of Enoch, Elijah, Jesus, the church and the 144,000 Jews in John's Revelation. It is very important to distinguish between the Rapture and the Second Coming.

The Rapture is the event when the church is caught up to meet Jesus in the air. The Second Coming is when Christ comes back to the earth to rule and reign for 1,000 years. These two separate events often get misunderstood in Scripture. Confusion comes when we mistakenly use a passage intended for one event and apply it to the other.

In this chapter, instead of dealing with the primary (or recognized) Rapture passages, we will look at text that is seldom read as a reference to the Rapture. In each of these instances, the prophetic layer of Scripture will allow us to see and unlock the prophecy code that has been laid out for us with types and shadows.

The Book of Remembrance

Then those who feared the Lord spoke to one another, and the Lord listened and heard them; so a book of remembrance was written before Him for those who fear the Lord and who meditate on His name. "They shall be Mine," says the Lord of hosts, "on the day that I make them My jewels. And I will spare them as a man spares his own son who serves him." Then you shall again discern between the righteous and the wicked, between one who serves God and one who does not serve Him (Malachi 3:16-18).

One of the interesting things about this text is that it precedes the verses introducing the Day of the Lord, the time when God comes to judge the earth. There is also a reference to the Rapture, immediately followed by a teaching on the Day of the Lord, a time we call the Great Tribulation that ends at Armageddon.

The passage begins by introducing the group, namely "those who feared the Lord." It informs us, first of all, that this group was talking to each other, and God was listening to the conversation. The last line of verse 16, "and who meditate on His name," lets us know they are redeemed. The name above every name is Jesus, so the transcriber of heaven writes a list of names—*the Book of Remembrance*—written in the presence of the Lord.

Revelation 13:8 refers to the *Book of Life*, where the names of *all* the redeemed have been recorded. Since the events in Revelation 13 take place during the Tribulation period, the Book of Life is still being written. As a matter of fact, it is the book that will be opened to judge all mankind at the Great White Throne Judgment. Therefore, the Book of Remembrance and the Book of Life cannot be one and the same.

Perhaps this group in Malachi, when speaking to one another, was fulfilling the scripture in 1 Thessalonians 4:16-18, which reads:

For the Lord Himself will descend from heaven with a shout, with the voice of an archangel, and with the trumpet of God. And the dead in Christ will rise first. Then we who are alive and remain shall be caught up together with them in the clouds to meet the Lord in the air. And thus we shall always be with the Lord. Therefore comfort one another with these words.

The Book of Remembrance in Malachi 3:16 seems to be for a group God calls His—the group He spares when He makes up, or gathers, His "jewels." The Book of Remembrance in Malachi 3:16 seems to be for a group God calls His—the group He spares when He makes up, or gathers, His "jewels." This group is gathered to distinguish between those who serve God and those who do not, and appears to be for an illustration to the earth. In the Parable of the Field (hidden treasure) in Matthew 13:44, a man finds a treasure and sells all that he has to buy the field, in order to have the treasure.

Since Jesus already interpreted the meaning of *the field* in the Parable of the Sower, we know the field represents the people of the world. He gave up His heavenly existence to come to earth, knowing that everyone would not believe in Him. Yet, the treasure in the field was worth enough for Him to give up all that He had. That parable identifies the jewels. The jewels are the believers who are gathered to be spared the coming judgment on the earth.

The Return of the Bride

> Come, and let us return to the Lord; for He has
> torn, but He will heal us; He has stricken, but He
> will bind us up. After two days He will revive
> us; on the third day He will raise us up, that we
> may live in His sight. Let us know, let us pursue
> the knowledge of the Lord. His going forth is
> established as the morning; He will come to us
> like the rain, like the latter and former rain to the
> earth (Hosea 6:1-3).

God already made it clear in the exegetical layer of
the Book of Hosea that Hosea's wayward wife is a
symbol of Israel following strange gods. Therefore,
the phrase "let us return to the Lord" is in reference
to Israel. The prophet is foretelling a day when Israel
will come back to God in the same way Hosea's wayward wife, Gomer, came back to him. Thus, the passage leaves no room for ambiguous interpretation.
However, all of a sudden it takes a dive into a deeper layer of scripture and veils itself in spiritual mystery. The next part of the text states that "after two
days He will revive us" and "on the third day He
will raise us up." Israel wasn't revived two days after
Hosea's prophecy, so the prophecy must have a
deeper meaning.

Peter is giving a lesson on the end times when he
makes this astonishing announcement in his second
epistle to the church:

> "Beloved, do not forget this one thing, that with
> the Lord one day is as a thousand years, and a

thousand years as one day. The Lord is not slack concerning His promise, as some count slackness, but is longsuffering toward us, not willing that any should perish but that all should come to repentance" (2 Peter 3:8, 9).

Many skeptics have tried to explain this phrase away as a generic reference to the timelessness of God. However, I believe it means exactly what it says.

When God created the earth, He made it in six days and rested on the seventh day. Was that necessary for an omnipotent God? Obviously, He could have made the world in one day or even one hour, if He had chosen to do so. God made the world in this fashion to set up the calendar of mankind. These six days actually depict six thousand years. The seventh day is the 7,000th year when the millennial reign of Christ will begin on this earth. It is the time prophesied by the writer in Hebrews 4 that there yet remains a rest for God's people and that we shall enter into that rest.

It is interesting that God commanded light on the first day, but He did not create the sun and moon until the fourth day. This too was part of His calendar for man. The fourth day would be the 4,000th year of man's existence—the year Jesus was born, the Light of the World.

The sun and moon are a type and shadow of Christ and His church.

The sun and moon are a type and shadow of Christ and His church. We know the moon is not even a light; it is only a reflection of the sun. Yet, the moon controls the tide of the ocean, which is the beginning of the life cycle for mankind. The tide creates the wind currents, cleanses the oceans and rules over the darkness. The church, too, is the beginning of new life for man. It creates the wind current through the power of the Holy Spirit, teaching truth to cleanse the earth (mankind) of impurity, and it has been given authority to rule over the darkness. We become a reflection of the Son.

We become a reflection of the Son.

Hosea's prophecy that Israel would be revived at the end of two days and raised up on the third is a prophecy concerning the times of the Gentiles. Peter declared on the Day of Pentecost that we were in the last days. How many days are there in the last days? The answer is only two. The last days is a reference to the last two days of the week of mankind's allotted 6,000 years.

The final day will be the seventh day and will usher in the last 1,000 year of man, known as the millennial reign of Christ on the earth. Note that after the first 2,000 years of mankind, the earth was destroyed by a flood. The second 2,000-year span—or 4,000th year— we saw the birth of Christ. Every 2,000 years, there is a significant supernatural change on the planet. As we near the end of the Gentile age, we are anticipating the rapture of the church and the Tribulation period so that we can begin the 1,000 years of rest and peace. Hosea declared that on the third day, they (meaning Israel) would be raised up. That promise is made many times to Israel concerning the reign of Messiah on the earth.

After reading the reference to *two days* and *three days*, it is more than coincidence that the next verse reads, "Let us know, let us pursue the knowledge of the Lord." It is as though He is leaving us a signpost to look for deeper spiritual meaning of this phrase.

"He will come to us like the rain" is a reference with two illustrations. The phrase refers to the former and latter rains. One, He will come from heaven, just like the rain. And two, as we have already discovered, the former and latter rains produced two harvests. The first rain produced the barley harvest, and the second rain produced the wheat harvest. The Parable of the Wheat and Tares (Matthew 13:24-30) tells us the wheat, referring to God's people, will be separated from the tares by the angels. These two illustrations point us to a time at the end of the age when Jesus will come back to the earth at the Second Coming to restore Israel.

Enter Your Chambers and Shut the Doors Behind You

As a woman with child is in pain and cries out in her pangs, when she draws near the time of her delivery, so have we been in Your sight, O Lord. We have been with child, we have been in pain; we have, as it were, brought forth wind; we have not accomplished any deliverance in the earth, nor have the inhabitants of the world fallen. Your dead shall live; together with my dead body they shall arise. Awake and sing, you who dwell in dust; for your dew is like the dew of herbs, and the earth shall cast out the dead. Come, my people, enter your chambers, and shut your doors behind you; hide yourself, as it were, for a little moment, until the indignation is past. For behold, the Lord comes out of His place to punish the inhabitants of the earth for their iniquity; the earth will also disclose her blood, and will no more cover her slain (Isaiah 26:17-21).

The passage opens with a woman in pain because of the labor pangs of childbirth. This is the same illustration given in 1 Thessalonians 5:1-4:

But concerning the times and the seasons, brethren, you have no need that I should write to you. For you yourselves know perfectly that the day of the Lord so comes as a thief in the night. For when they say, "Peace and safety!" then sudden destruction comes upon them, as labor pains upon a pregnant woman. And they shall not escape. But you, brethren, are not in darkness, so that this Day should overtake you as a thief.

The illustration of the woman about to give birth is given to help us understand the timing of the Lord's return. Even though no one knows the day or the hour of a delivery time, we can see the signs of childbirth increasing as we get near the time of delivery. The same is true with the signs of the time.

In Isaiah 26, we are told that even though we are pregnant with signs and expectation, nothing has been born up to now. But then all at once, the prophet opens his mouth and declares, "Your dead shall live; together with my dead body they shall arise. Awake and sing, you who dwell in dust. . . ." The prophet of God is declaring a day of resurrection. He proclaims that the earth shall cast out its dead. He doesn't just leave us with the notion of a resurrection of the dead, but gives a time frame as well.

The next phrase is "Come, my people." These are the words John heard as he stood upon the isle of Patmos. John's physical rapture from Patmos to heaven came after he saw an open door, heard the sound of a trumpet, and a voice that said, "Come up here" (Revelation 4:1).

Take Refuge From the Coming Judgment

Come, my people, enter your chambers,
And shut your doors behind you;
Hide yourself, as it were, for a little moment,
Until the indignation is past (Isaiah 26:20).

This is indeed a Rapture passage. It speaks of a place of refuge during the time of tribulation on the earth. It tells us to enter our chambers, shut the doors behind us, and stay there for a moment until the indignation is past. These words echo the preceding phrase about the resurrection of the dead. It is Isaiah's version of 1 Thessalonians 4:16, 17:

For the Lord Himself will descend from heaven with a shout, with the voice of an archangel, and with the trumpet of God. And the dead in Christ will rise first. Then we who are alive and remain shall be caught up together with them in the clouds to meet the Lord in the air. And thus we shall always be with the Lord.

The final verse of the text says that as the dead are raised and the righteous enter their chambers of refuge, the Lord will come out from His place and bring vengeance on the people of the earth for their sins.

THE STORY OF ESTHER

A Type of the Bride of Christ

The story of Queen Esther is an intriguing story from many angles. From the Jewish perspective, it gives hope and a reason to celebrate deliverance from Israel's enemies. From the exegetical layer of Scripture, it tells an encouraging story of how an adopted girl became the queen and saved a nation from its enemy. That should be inspiration enough for us to read this captivating and heart-wrenching story. However, if we dig into the prophetic layer where God overlaid types and shadows to tell of a greater spiritual truth, we will find that we, too, are part of the story of Esther.

There are so many Scripture references for this that I will only refer to them rather than print all of them. I encourage you to read each passage as we work through the prophetic layer of this story.

Esther 1:10-12

The Book of Esther opens up with the declaration of a seven-day feast. The story gets most interesting when the seven days are ended. *Seven* is the number of completion and with it, we are given our first sign to look for type and shadow codes that will unlock a prophetic truth. At the end of the seven days, Queen Vashti was presented before the king and she refused his request. The king decided to banish her from the kingdom and pursue his search for an obedient bride.

While Queen Vashti was not Jewish, she does represent the nation of Israel—the nation of covenant and the apple of God's eye that rejected the Messiah at His first coming.

While Queen Vashti was not Jewish, she does represent the nation of Israel—the nation of covenant and the apple of God's eye that rejected the Messiah at His first coming. God told the prophet Daniel that because of Israel's rejection, He would raise up the Gentiles, and after their time had ended, He would give Israel seven more years to repent and be restored to Messiah. Esther 1:19 tells us the queen will come no more before the king, and her position will be given to another. That is how Esther became the bride of a king, and that is precisely how Christ's church will become the bride.

Esther 2:7, 17, 18

In the introduction of Esther in this text, we are told that she was adopted. Romans 8:15 reads that the only way Gentiles got into the family was through adoption. Esther was chosen to be a candidate for purification in much the same way that God chose us and began to purify our lives for His service.

The next two chapters in the book relate how Esther dealt with her enemies. As the church, we are not only called to be in the family of God, but we are also called to be in the army of God. As soldiers, we fight the good fight of faith, warring against our Enemy until our Lord's return.

Esther 5:1, 2

In Esther's desperation to rescue the Jewish people, she decides to conquer their enemies once and for all. Chapter 5 of the book begins by saying "on the third day," she put on her royal robes and went into the throne room of the king. We have already discussed the prophetic significance of the third day. Esther's dressing in her royal garments on the third day is a type of the rapture of the church. Once robed, she then entered the inner court of the king's chambers and stood waiting for him to call her up.

Esther's dressing in her royal garments on the third day is a type of the rapture of the church.

The inner court of the Tabernacle and sanctuary was where the priests ministered before the Lord. Women were not allowed in the inner court, so Esther took her very life into her own hands with this action. As children of God, we have entered into the priesthood of all believers and minister in the Word, worship, prayers and works of the Holy Spirit, which are foreshadowed in the furnishings of the inner court.

Esther faced the entrance to the king's house. The entrance to the house of the Lord was always represented by facing east toward Jerusalem. We, the church, are told to look toward the eastern sky for our redemption. Esther found favor in the sight of the king and was called to enter his house and place her hand upon his scepter. Esther in her royal garments, facing the house of the king and receiving the call to enter, is a beautiful portrait of the Rapture. Her enemies are not yet defeated. The plan to overthrow the enemy takes place in the king's house at a banquet. The evil man, Haman, who plotted to kill all of the Jews in one day, is instead killed on that appointed day. The Jewish people are not only free, but they are honored and all of their enemies are destroyed. The story ends with the Jews having their property restored to them and being able to rebuild their lands.

Likewise, the church attends the wedding feast, or banquet, called the Marriage Supper of the Lamb, while the Enemy is being defeated on the earth. In the story of the church, our enemies are also defeated, and we come back to the earth to rebuild it, along with restored Israel.

This beautiful story tells how a king married an adopted Jewish girl, defeated her enemies, called her into his house, and restored her nation. It is a type and shadow of the story of the church in that it tells how an adopted people, engrafted into the Jewish vine, marries the King of kings, who defeats our Enemy with His decree and restores our nation.

Questions for Discussion

1. Is the Rapture one end-time event? Explain.

2. Discuss the difference, if any, between the Rapture and the Second Coming.

3. Name and discuss three Rapture patterns established in Scripture.

4. For whom is the Book of Remembrance written?

5. Explain the Parable of the Field (or hidden treasure).

6. In God's economy of time, what significance does the creation of the sun and moon on the fourth day have in relation to the birth of Christ?

7. Explain the latter and the former rain reference in Hosea 6:3.

8. In the story of Esther, what is the significance of the number *seven*?

9. How is Esther's placement into her family indicative of the church?

10. Explain Esther's third-day events as they reveal future events.

This is the history of the heavens and the earth

when they were created . . .

before any plant of the field was in the earth

and before any herb of the field had grown.

For the Lord God had not caused it to rain

on the earth, and there was no man to till the ground;

but a mist went up from the earth and watered

the whole face of the ground. And the Lord

God formed man of the dust of the ground,

and breathed into his nostrils the breath of life;

and man became a living being

(Genesis 2:4-7).

10

JESUS IN THE GARDEN

A t first glance, you may think this chapter is about the Garden of Gethsemane, but it is about the Garden of Eden. Man's physical origin began in the Garden of Eden, and our spiritual origin began there as well.

Before we get into the Genesis passage, we must understand that the apostle Paul calls Jesus the Second Adam ("last Adam") in 1 Corinthians 15. This term is used to describe the natures of the carnal and the spiritual man. However, we must not discount the fact that the Holy Spirit through the pen of the apostle was leaving us clues to search deeper into the Scriptures to better understand the ways of the Lord. As I mentioned before, our God is truly a God of precision. Given that, we have to go back to uncover the introduction of Adam to see how the origin of his character foreshadows the life of our Lord.

This is the history of the heavens and the earth when they were created . . . before any plant of the field was in the earth and before any herb of the field had grown. For the Lord God had not caused it to rain on the earth, and there was no man to till the ground; but a mist went up from the earth and watered the whole face of the ground. And the Lord God formed man of the dust of the ground, and breathed into his nostrils the breath of life; and man became a living being (Genesis 2:4-7).

Spiritual Decoder Keys

To understand this passage in the prophetic layer, we revisit the parables in Matthew 13. Jesus gave us the spiritual interpretations of only two parables: the Parable of the Sower and the Parable of the Wheat and the Tares. These parables contain spiritual decoder keys that help us to unlock the prophecy codes in other passages. Every scripture does not contain a prophetic code. But when we begin to see a pattern developing in a passage, we can apply the decoder keys to see if the passage passes the test of holding a type-and-shadow code of a future event.

In both parables, the field represents the human race. If we apply this key to Genesis 2:4-7, we see that the ground represents the human race. It also declares that God had not caused it to rain on the earth yet, because there was no man to till the ground. So far, we have a human race without the power and presence of the Holy Spirit operating through them, because there was no spiritual gardener.

Since we understand that the outpouring of the former and latter rains in the Bible represent two different outpourings of the Holy Spirit, we can also add this to the keys. The gardener to till the ground is also identified for us in the parables of Matthew 13. The man is Jesus, who was portrayed as the Sower and also the Owner of the field in the interpretation of the Parable of theWheat and the Tares. Instead of rain, a mist went up from the earth to water it. The mist

The man is Jesus, who was portrayed as the Sower and also the Owner of the field in the interpretation of the Parable of the Wheat and the Tares.

is symbolic of the work of the Holy Spirit, as water is a symbol of the Spirit, but it was not yet poured out on the field. The mist represents a type of the Holy Spirit through the ministry of the priests and prophets in the first Testament.

We are told in verse 7 that God formed man out of the ground. Using the decoder keys—the ground represents the human race. This means that God made a Man from the human race—Jesus, born of a virgin and conceived by the Holy Ghost. Reading the passage carefully, we find that Adam was made from the "dust of the ground." It was part of the soil, but not completely soil. The word translated as *dust* is the same word translated *clay*. The consistency of clay is a combination of dirt and water. The man made from the earth was given breath.

While all living things breathe, the Bible only records that God gave breath to the man in the Garden. The word *breath* is synonymous with *spirit*. The descriptive words that accompany the word *breath* are *life* and *giving*. This life-giving breath denotes much more than just lung expansion and oxygen flow to the body. The life-giving breath was not just air—it was the breath of God. John tells us that God is Spirit, and we must worship Him in spirit and in truth (4:24).

God breathing into the man is more than mouth-to-mouth resuscitation. It is God, who is Spirit, giving a part of Himself to the man. Man received his spirit when God breathed it into him. On the exegetical layer of the scripture, this is the story of the first Adam, who is the father of the human race. On the prophetic layer, it is the story of Jesus coming to the world—the Spirit/Man who has within Him a spiritual breath that gives life just by speaking the words.

> The Lord God planted a garden eastward in Eden, and there He put the man whom He had formed. And out of the ground the Lord God made every tree grow that is pleasant to the sight and good for food. The tree of life was also in the midst of the garden, and the tree of the knowledge of good and evil. Now a river went out of Eden to water the garden, and from there it parted and became four riverheads (Genesis 2:8-10).

In the prophetic layer, the Garden of Eden and the trees in it represent the nation of Israel and Jerusalem in particular. It is the place God chose to build the Temple and dwell with man in the Holy Place. Just as we discussed in an earlier chapter, again we see Jerusalem symbolic of the Garden of Eden. Solomon's temple was the first building that housed a visible presence of God on the earth. Of course, this does not take into consideration the tabernacle of Moses, which was a cloth building or tent, designed for mobility. The Garden is not the whole world. It is a special place or home God created for Adam. It is a place filled with good trees.

Jesus gave us the parable of the trees that bear good fruit and the ones that do not. These trees were symbols of people. The nation of Israel is also symbolized by an image of the fig tree. We can conclude that the trees in the Garden are symbolic of people as well. In this Garden of fruit-bearing trees, there are two specific trees mentioned:

1. The Tree of Life

2. The Tree of Knowledge of Good and Evil

The two trees symbolize the two natures of man and the two paths man must choose. The Tree of Life represents Jesus and the life He brings to the world. The other is the Tree of Knowledge. While knowledge of good and evil is a good thing, it can also keep people from the Tree of Life.

Knowledge is only as good as its source. Of itself, knowledge is only partial enlightenment. However, many people serve the god of knowledge, and believe what their senses reveal to them as though it were truth. This type of knowledge leads to humanism. *Humanism* is a science that believes the human is the highest form of the evolutionary process. The philosophy of humanism is based on the concept of knowledge. This type of carnal knowledge leaves no room for faith or spirituality. The tree represents man's choice to serve himself instead of God. It isn't necessarily representative of Satan, who disguised himself as a serpent in the Garden.

Few people today claim allegiance to Satan as their master. However, countless billions have chosen to serve themselves and knowledge, rather than serve God. Satan uses this deceit of self-centered thinking to trick people into doing his bidding in the name of self-gain, self-preservation and self-centeredness.

The deceit of knowledge still blinds much of the human race from the only tree that can bring them life—the Tree of Life.

Many people believe they are self-made—that they have earned their own way through life and deserve everything they can take. These same people view God as a sideline hobby for people who need some sort of crutch to get them through life. The deceit of knowledge still blinds much of the human race from the only tree that can bring them life—the Tree of Life.

The Garden of Eden had four riverheads that flowed out of the Garden. The indication is that each of these rivers originate in the Garden. The running water is a prophetic type of the Holy Spirit in Acts 2, which originates in Jerusalem and is poured out to the four corners of the earth.

> And the Lord God said, "It is not good that man should be alone; I will make him a helper comparable to him" (Genesis 2:18).

God decided to create a bride for Adam, one who would be a companion to him and assist him with his work. Adam had dominion over everything in the Garden. He was in charge of naming the animals, as well as helping to till the Garden of God. This is a shadow of the church, which is called the bride of Christ. Paul gave the illustration of a married couple as a metaphor of Christ and the church. The word *helper* used in this passage is the same as the Greek word *parakletos*, which can be translated *helper* or *comforter* in the English language. This word is also used to describe the Holy Spirit that would later come and indwell man.

The Holy Spirit restored the "dead" spirit of man and gave him life in Christ. The indwelling of the Holy Spirit makes us spiritually alive. It is the only way we can be His bride, since it is a spiritual matrimony, and not one of flesh. We are indeed Christ's helpers on this earth. As we fulfill the Great Commission and do the works of Him who has sent

The indwelling of the Holy Spirit makes us spiritually alive.

us, we are indeed being the companion of the Second Adam, the spiritual man (1 Corinthians 15:44-49).

> Out of the ground the Lord God formed every beast of the field and every bird of the air, and brought them to Adam to see what he would call them. And whatever Adam called each living creature, that was its name. So Adam gave names to all cattle, to the birds of the air, and to every beast of the field. But for Adam there was not found a helper comparable to him (Genesis 2:19, 20).

This part of the story seems to be a parenthetical statement. While it is a part of the Creation story, it takes us on somewhat of a side road from our story of Adam and Eve. Even though a bit disconnected, it does remind us of the plight of the human struggle between wickedness and spirituality. Man must make a choice to serve God. The beasts and the birds remind us of our double nature: natural and spiritual. They remind us that we are always surrounded by spiritual influences and those that deter us from our spiritual walk by enticing us to serve our carnal nature. The beasts and the birds are the dual roads of life, and we can only choose one.

The beasts and the birds remind us of our double nature: natural and spiritual.

Since the ground represents the human race, it is important to notice that God has now made two other species out of the ground. There is no mention of sea creatures, insects, reptiles or other species made from the ground. God *spoke* these other species into existence, so why did He take the time to make birds and cattle out of the ground? On the exegetical layer, this makes no sense at all. However, on the prophetic layer, it does make sense.

Cattle are used for the next few hundred years as sacrifices for the sins of man. Only two kinds of birds are acceptable sacrifices—turtledoves and pigeons—and they are not prepared for the sacrifice in the same way as cattle. The birds were only acceptable sacrifices when offered by the poorest of people who could not afford to own cattle and, even then, only accepted in certain circumstances. The cattle are separated a certain way, but not the birds. This is significant since Jesus interprets the birds in the Parable of the Sower as "the wicked one." This could be Satan, or any wicked person used by him to steal the seed of the Word from your life. Since the cattle are the acceptable sacrifices, they represent the righteous people in the earth.

The birds represent the wicked people. Perhaps the two species of birds represent those who live a wicked life but repent just before they die. They are permitted to enter heaven as a child of God, but lose their reward and crowns, since they did not serve Him on earth. Entrance to heaven is free to all who come under the blood of Jesus, but rewards, honors, titles and crowns are earned through laboring for Him while on the earth. In the same way that Adam was given the task of naming the animals as part of being the lord of the Garden, we are told in the Book of Revelation that we, too, will be given a new name in heaven when Jesus Christ presents us to the Father.

> And the Lord God caused a deep sleep to fall on Adam, and he slept; and He took one of his ribs, and closed up the flesh in its place. Then the rib which the Lord God had taken from man He made into a woman, and He brought her to the man (Genesis 2:21, 22).

If God can create a universe with His voice, then each time He does something unique, it is our responsibility to try and understand the clues He has given us to unlock the prophecy code.

If God can create a universe with His voice, then each time He does something unique, it is our responsibility to try and understand the clues He has given us to unlock the prophecy code. Up to this point in Genesis, the Creator has created most things with the spoken word. Although He did form Adam out of the ground, in verse 22 He did something completely different— He created a woman from the rib of Adam. Knowing the nature and abilities of the creative powers of God, this was certainly an unusual way to introduce us to Eve. There must be a higher spiritual purpose in the way He chose to create her.

Since we are looking at Adam as a type of Christ, we must look into this deep sleep that God caused to come on him. This sleep can be likened to the death of

Christ on the cross. In the teachings of the apostle Paul in 1 Corinthians and 1 Thessalonians, he refers to death as *sleep*. Another clue to this prophetic code is found in John 10:17, 18:

> "Therefore My Father loves Me, because I lay down My life that I may take it again. No one takes it from Me, but I lay it down of Myself. I have power to lay it down, and I have power to take it again. This command I have received from My Father."

Jesus being the God-man could not die spiritually. He laid down His life, but He was only dead physically. Spiritually, He was fully alive, aware and alert. Genesis 2:21 tells us that God took one of Adam's ribs and made a woman. This is symbolic of God forming the *bride* of Christ out of the *body* of Christ. When Jesus died on the cross, the soldier pierced His side, just under the rib cage. The Bible records that out of His side flowed blood and water. These are the same visible substances that flow from the natural birth canal when a baby is born.

In verse 21, the term "one of his ribs" is interesting, as if God wanted us to see which one was taken. Humans have 12 pairs of ribs, and each pair extends from one of the thoracic vertebrae. The vertebrae are the 33 individual bones of the backbone or spinal column. The upper seven pairs of ribs, called true ribs, are connected to the breastbone. The remaining five pairs below the true ribs are called false ribs. The upper three pairs of false ribs are attached to the backbone, and each of these ribs is connected to the cartilage of the rib above it. The last two pairs of false ribs are smaller than the other ribs and are called floating ribs because they are attached only to the backbone and not to the breastbone or any other rib. The way God designed the rib cage of man may seem immaterial, until we look at this unusual formation from the prophetic layer.

Number Patterns in Scripture

In order to understand the rib equation and clues left to us by God, we need to review a few of the number patterns in Scripture that help us understand Biblical types and shadows.

❶ *Two* is the number of Jesus. We can understand this in many ways. He is the Second Adam, the second person of the Trinity, and the spiritual man the Bible says is second, not first (1 Corinthians 15:46).

❶ *Twelve* is the number of government. God chose to establish the nation of Israel from 12 tribes. Jesus chose to form the church from 12 apostles. There are 24 elders mentioned in heaven representing the 12 of the first and second Testaments. The first 12 are for Israel and the second 12 are for the Gentile church.

❶ *Seven* is the number of completion for things on the earth. God completed the Creation in seven days. The Tribulation is seven years to complete the time of judgment. In the story of Joseph, Pharaoh's dream of the seven cows and the seven heads of grain represent seven years to complete the years of plenty and the years of famine. There are numerous illustrations in Scripture that help us understand this prophetic pattern.

❶ *Five* is the number of grace. Grace is a free gift from God, that which is unmerited or not earned. God made the world in five days and gave it to Adam on the sixth day. God established the Law in the five books of Moses, called the Pentateuch or Torah. God established the priesthood with five priests— Aaron and his four sons. In Jerusalem by the sheep market was the Pool of Bethesda, having five porches, where the angel came and stirred up the water to give the gift of healing. God established the church with a fivefold ministry of grace. There are numerous other examples.

❶ *Three* is the number of divine completion. We have already discussed the third-day principle which correlates with this truth of divine completion.

Using the application of the prophetic numeric system, let us review the formation of the rib cage once again:

1. There are the 33 vertebrae that hold it all together. Jesus was 33 years old when He was crucified.

2. There are 12 pairs of ribs, making a total of 24—12 ribs for Israel and 12 for the church.

3. There are seven pairs of attached ribs called the true ribs, which represent the completed work of God among the Jews and also the Gentiles.

4. Below those are five more ribs on each side called the false ribs. These represent the grace given to the Jews and also to the Gentiles.

5. As a part of the five false ribs, there are three ribs attached to the other ribs. Since *three* is the number of divine completion, we understand that the story of the rib cage is telling us that through the completed works on the earth (number 7) and the works of grace (number 5), God completes His divine plan in the Jews and Gentiles by joining them together through the life of Christ (via the 33 vertebrae) and making them a part of one body, the Lord's body.

6. All we have left now are the two pairs of floating ribs. Although they are not attached to any of the other ribs, these two pairs are connected to the backbone, *two* being the number representing Jesus, who was born of the woman (a

rib) but was also God (detached). As the God-
man, He was both physical and spiritual at the
same time. Two of the floating ribs are for
Israel because He is their Messiah, something
they will eventually come to understand. The
other two ribs are for the Gentiles who make
up the church. Both are connected to Him.

I believe the rib taken from Adam's side to form his
bride was one of the two floating ribs. It is not until the
rib is taken that it becomes the bride, in the same way
that the church does not become the bride until it is
taken. The taking of the rib by God not only gives us
a portrait of the bride, but also of the Rapture. The taking of the rib from the rest of the ribs is the rapture of
the church from the rest of the world. We can go a step
further, by using the passage in Job that speaks of God
working on the left hand and the right hand. We
know that when He works on the left hand, we do not
understand what He is doing, but the right hand is the
hand of power. Jesus is seated at the right hand of God
interceding for the saints. Using the right and left
hands of a man as a reference, we can conclude that
the right side is the church and the left side is Israel
who does not yet understand the full plan, because
God is still working on the left side.

Much research has been conducted into the historical practice of crucifixion. Medical experts tend to
agree because of access to the right ventricle, and the
description that "blood and water flowed" that it was

the right side of Christ's body that was pierced with the spear. If this is correct, we can conclude that the rib that was removed from Adam was the bottom floating rib on his right side, which is a type and shadow of the raptured church and bride of Christ.

> And Adam said: "This is now bone of my bones and flesh of my flesh; she shall be called Woman, because she was taken out of Man." Therefore a man shall leave his father and mother and be joined to his wife, and they shall become one flesh. And they were both naked, the man and his wife, and were not ashamed (Genesis 2:23-25).

Eve is called *woman*, which is a derivative of a Hebrew word also used for *man*. The word indicates that her origin was from the man. In the same way, we, the bride of Christ, came from the body of Christ and thus are called Christians. Adam declares that she is flesh of his flesh and bone of his bone. Our union with Christ is not physical, but spiritual, and He declared over us that we are one with Him (John 17:22, 23). We are not flesh and blood, but we are one in spirit, since the same Spirit that dwells in Christ is now also in us (see Romans 8:9-11).

We are not flesh and blood, but we are one in spirit, since the same Spirit that dwells in Christ is now also in us (see Romans 8:9-11).

Subsequently, we are told that because woman was taken from man, a man should leave his father and mother and be joined to his wife. Since it is our father and mother who made our physical bodies, and Christ who gave us spiritual life, we are being told to separate from our fleshly carnal nature in order to become spiritual. While we cannot take that statement literally, we must live by the example of our Lord who put His flesh to death that He might bring us spiritual life. That is why the apostle Paul said, "I have been crucified with Christ; it is no longer I who live, but Christ lives in me; and the life which I now live in the flesh I live by faith in the Son of God, who loved me and gave Himself for me" (Galatians 2:20).

How can we become one flesh with Christ as Adam and Eve became one flesh? Genesis 4:1 says, "Now Adam knew Eve his wife, and she conceived and bore Cain, and said, 'I have acquired a man from the Lord.' " The act of intimacy is referred to as *knowing the other person*. The word for *knew* is the Hebrew word *yada*. It is the root word for *yadah*, a word we see over 120 times in Scripture. *Yadah* is the same as the word *Judah* in English. It literally means "to give thanks and praise unto the Lord by extending our hands toward Him." Adam knew Eve through physical intimacy because he is the man of the flesh. We know Christ through spiritual intimacy because He is the spiritual man. Spiritual intimacy happens in the atmosphere of worship—yadah!

Through intense worship we move through levels of spiritual intimacy. In the Bible, the Song of Solomon is a book regarding intimacy that reveals three levels of

Through intense worship we move through levels of spiritual intimacy.

intimacy in the relationship between the Shulamite woman and the Shepherd. She goes looking for him three times. The first time when asked whom she is seeking, she replied, "My beloved." The second time they ask her, she replied, "My lover." The third time when asked whom she seeks, she replied, "My friend." It progresses from courtship, to a lover's honeymoon, to a place of trust, intimacy and truly "knowing" the other person. He is now her friend.

In Hosea 1:2, the Lord instructed the prophet to "take a wife of harlotry," which he did in obedience to God. In spite of affording her the rights and respect of being his wife, she went astray and ended up in slavery. In spite of Gomer's wrongs and flagrant betrayal of the relationship, again, in obedience to God, Hosea paid the purchase price and bought her back from the auction block. In following the prophetic layer, it is an obvious type and shadow of the intimate relationship between God and man. In John 15:16, Jesus declares: "You did not choose Me, but I chose you."

In the Garden of Eden, God and the first Adam share a pure intimacy in the spirit. Then sin worms its way into the heart of Adam's bride, and they trade the Tree of Life for the Tree of Knowledge of Good and Evil. Through the first Adam, all of mankind is trapped in the slavery of sin, self and Satan until the Second Adam—Jesus the Bridegroom—paid the purchase price and bought us back from the auction block so that we could call Him "Master!"

However, He didn't purchase us to be His servants. He paid the price because we are His bride. The Lord says in Hosea 2:19, 20, "I will betroth you to Me forever; yes, I will betroth you to Me in righteousness and justice, in lovingkindness and mercy; I will betroth you to Me in faithfulness, and you shall know the Lord." Just as in the Song of Solomon, the relationship progresses to a place of trust, intimacy and truly "knowing" the other person. He is now *our* Friend.

Jesus says in John 15:11-15:

> "These things I have spoken to you, that My joy may remain in you, and that your joy may be full. This is My commandment, that you love one another as I have loved you. Greater love has no one than this, than to lay down one's life for his friends. You are My friends if you do whatever I command you. No longer do I call you servants, for a servant does not know what his master is doing; but I have called you friends, for all things that I heard from My Father I have made known to you."

The concealed is revealed to us by Christ in His interpretation of the two parables. He gave us the keys to unlock the prophecy code. All glory to God!

Questions for Discussion

1. True or false: Man's physical origin began in the Garden of Eden, and his spiritual origin began in the Garden of Gethsemane. Defend your answer.

2. In the decoded parables, what represents the human race?

3. What does the breath of God impart into man?

4. What do the trees in the Garden of Eden symbolize in man?

5. *Five* is the number of grace. Name five prophetic examples.

6. Discuss the symbolism of Eve being formed from a rib taken from Adam's side.

7. Explain the types in the prophetic layer that are represented by the numeric intricacies of the human rib cage.

8. What is the prophetic significance of Hosea and Gomer?

9. Name the three levels of intimacy in relationship.

10. How is intimacy relevant to understanding our spiritual relationship with Jesus?